Henry Nutcombe Oxenham

Dr. Pusey's Eirenicon considered in Relation to Catholic Unity

A Letter to the Rev. Father Lockhart of the Institute of Charity

Henry Nutcombe Oxenham

Dr. Pusey's Eirenicon considered in Relation to Catholic Unity
A Letter to the Rev. Father Lockhart of the Institute of Charity

ISBN/EAN: 9783337107185

Printed in Europe, USA, Canada, Australia, Japan

Cover: Foto ©ninafisch / pixelio.de

More available books at **www.hansebooks.com**

DR. PUSEY'S EIRENICON

CONSIDERED IN RELATION TO

CATHOLIC UNITY.

A LETTER

TO

THE REV. FATHER LOCKHART

OF THE INSTITUTE OF CHARITY.

BY

HENRY NUTCOMBE OXENHAM, M.A.

LATE SCHOLAR OF BALLIOL COLLEGE, OXFORD.

Second · Edition.

LONDON:
R. WASHBOURNE, 18A, PATERNOSTER ROW.
1871.

Propter fratres meos et proximos meos loquebar pacem de te :
Propter domum Domini Dei nostri quæsivi bona tibi.

PREFACE TO THE SECOND EDITION.

If it cannot be said that the interest roused by the remarkable work which suggested this publication has passed away, as indeed is evidenced by the subsequent issue of two supplementary volumes, still less certainly can the subject itself be considered to have lost its pressing and paramount claims on the attention of all religious minds. The position both of Catholics and Anglicans, and their relations to each other, are in some respects different from what they were five years ago, and circumstances, which it would be out of place to enter upon here, may seem for the moment to have widened the gulf between them. But man's necessity is God's opportunity, and the very difficulties which look so formidable may eventually become, under His good Providence, the prelude to a better understanding. Meanwhile, nothing has occurred during the last five years, to shake the estimate of facts conveyed in the following pages, while later experience has served very strongly to confirm the inferences deduced from them. Some points might, no doubt, have been differently treated, were the Letter being written now, but the author has seen no ground for abandoning the convictions it expresses; and to remodel it in the light of subsequent events would, in fact, be simply to re-write it. The treatise therefore reappears in its original shape, in compliance with suggestions which have been made to him, and in the hope of its recuring the same kindly reception accorded to the previous issue, from many various quarters.

He would seize this occasion for recalling attention to a point frequently dwelt upon in the course of the argument, and which has been more and more forcing itself of late on the consideration of thoughtful and earnest believers, at present unhappily separated from one another. And that is the daily increasing pressure of the common enemy on the outworks of what should be the citadel of our common faith. "If," to quote the words of the most learned of the French Bishops, "a thinly disguised atheism ravages even Christian lands, doubt not that one of the most powerful causes of these moral and social miseries, these shameful humiliations, lies in the unhappy internal divisions among Christians. If the Oriental Churches, and our brethren separated from unity by the violent revolutions of the sixteenth century, were reunited with us, what a new power of transformation and victory would Christianity display in the world, bringing into one focus all the living forces of progress, science and civilization." And it is not a little significant that the eloquent words of the Catholic Prelate should be reechoed in a state paper, issued last year by the Protestant Prussian Government, which speaks of a tendency manifesting itself, "which encourages us to hope the day may come when all the living forces of Christianity will be reunited in a common resistance to the errors at present prevailing in the world, to the great detriment of religion."

Truly "there is thunder on the horizon as well as dawn;" τὸ δ'εὖ νικάτω.

LETTER.

My dear Father Lockhart,

The friendship which has now subsisted between us for about nine years, commencing when I was still an Anglican, might perhaps be a sufficient excuse for my seeking the permission you have so kindly accorded me to address to yourself some considerations suggested by the appearance and character of the remarkable work named on my title-page, which has so deeply stirred the religious sympathies of a large portion of our countrymen, as also of foreign Catholics, and bids fair to form an epoch in the history of English theology and of the National Church.

But I had, in fact, further reasons besides that of personal friendship for desiring to address you. Though you were one of the earliest converts, and can reckon more years of priesthood than some who are already preparing to say their first mass can reckon years of life, you have never ceased to take a keen and kindly interest in the great movement commenced some thirty years ago at Oxford, which has exerted and continues to exert so wide and so various an influence over the literature, the thought, the religion, and the policy of England. You have never sneered at the Catholic aspirations, or ignored the conscientious difficulties, or slighted the doctrinal approximations, or laughed at the ritual developments, or mistrusted the sincerity, or discredited the zeal, or repelled the friendly advances of those without our pale, but who in heart, even when they know it not, are often very near us. And, more than that, you were (I believe) the first among us to call the attention of English Catholics to Dr. Pusey's recent work in two very striking papers, published originally in the 'Weekly Register,' which elicited a prompt and cordial response from the author himself, and have since been noticed, as yours, with respectful commendation, by the leading organ of the French Jesuits, as also by the High Church Quarterly in this country.* While, therefore, I have no right to assume beforehand your agreement in everything I may say, still less to make you responsible for it, I have good ground for hoping that in the main your sympathies will be with me, and that you will be ready to listen even where you may hesitate to assent.

It may perhaps be asked why I should speak at all, when elder and better men have already taken

---

* See the first of three remarkable articles on the *Eirenicon* in the *Études Religieuses* for January of this year (which Dr. Pusey has quoted with satisfaction in a letter to the *Guardian*); and a review of the book in the *Christian Remembrancer* for January. I shall have to refer to them further by-and-bye.

up the matter, and one especially, who has a preeminent right to be the spokesman of English Catholics, has handled it with even more than his usual felicity? Certainly not with any view of criticising or controverting what they have said, still less of putting myself in comparison with them. But if questions so vast in their scope, so manifold in their ramifications, so momentous in their bearings, are to be raised at all, it is only after the fullest and freest ventilation that any practical result can be looked for. The final decision must, of course, rest with authority; but, as we have been lately reminded, 'in matters which may happen to be in debate, ecclesiastical authority watches the state of opinion, and the direction and course of controversy, and decides accordingly.' * To that authority it must be left, in the words of the Jesuit reviewer mentioned just now, 'to welcome or reject the advances of the Anglican Church.' He adds : 'Quant à nous, le seul rôle qui nous convienne c'est de laisser raconter les faits, sans prétendre nous poser en juges des conditions ou des propositions de paix.' † And in the previous discussion, which is the first requisite for an ultimate adjustment, it is open to all to take part who are really interested in the question, and on some points at least have had fair opportunity for arriving at deliberate convictions. Nor does it at all follow because their opinion may not always be

---

* Ne man's *Letter on Eirenicon*, p. 21.
† *Études Religieuses*, No. 37, p. 137.

right, that there is no advantage in stating it. Mistaken or inadequate judgments often have their use, and in practical matters incidental error is almost a condition of eventual success. It cannot, then, be other than a gain that as many cross-lights, so to say, should be thrown on the discussion as possible, from varieties of experience, temperament, habit, or mental constitution in individuals; so long as they speak in good faith, with due regard to the feelings of others, and with deference to authority.

And I may venture to put forward one plea for a hearing not shared by yourself and others who are my superiors in position and learning and my elders in the Church, from the very circumstance of my conversion to Catholicism being more recent, and my having as an Anglican belonged to a later and somewhat different phase of the movement in which they formerly bore so prominent a part. As the position and prospects of the Anglican Church did not probably present themselves to my mind, when I belonged to it, in quite the same light as to those who viewed it from the standpoint of early Tractarianism, it is only natural that in looking back upon it now my estimate of its present condition should not always precisely coincide with theirs. This remark is made with special reference to two questions not directly introduced into the 'Eirenicon' but which have been mooted in connection with it—the effects of the recent Privy Council judgments and the attitude of the Liberal party in the Church of England on the Anglican position, and what is called the Ritual Question. A brief notice of these points will bring me to the proper subject of my letter.

As regards the former, this is not the place to enter on an examination of the doctrines at issue in the Gorham case or the case of Essays and Reviews. Neither am I concerned here with the legitimate bearing of either decision on the conscientious position of individual Anglicans in their own communion. But looking at the matter *ab extra*, and with a view to possibilities of future reunion, it does not appear to me by any means an unmixed evil, that a body to which Anglicans themselves attribute no infallibility, and which *we* do not regard as possessing any authority at all in controversies of faith, should not have been officially committed to fresh definitions, at least on the subtle and difficult questions involved in the Essay and Review case, definitions which would almost certainly have required to be revised or explained quite as much as the 39 Articles, before they could be accepted as a basis of reunion. Of the three opinions which the Court refused to enforce, it must be remembered that one, as stated by them, is a heresy, and another an open question. The Lutheran dogma of imputed righteousness is expressly condemned by the Council of Trent; verbal inspiration has never been defined by the Church, and is probably held in our own day by very few theologians. The Gorham case was a simpler one, and more capable of being settled by ecclesiastical precedent; but

however objectionable the decision, its actual result is generally admitted to have been a widely increased reception of the doctrine impugned among both clergy and laity. Now I am very far from saying that 'omnigenous latitudinarianism' is to be tolerated in the Church; but I do certainly think that in dealing with an isolated and unauthoritative communion, which its warmest adherents must admit to be at best in an abnormal and transitional state, it is far more important to gauge the extent and vitality of the Catholic movement, both doctrinal and practical, among its members, than the formal character of the theological judgments of its courts. It matters comparatively little, as *we* regard the situation, how far the Anglican communion in its present state satisfies the proper ideal of 'a teaching Church;' but it does matter a good deal how far a Catholic standard is growingly recognised in the instruction given from its pulpits and the religious life of its people.*
It is under this last aspect mainly that we consider it an effective 'breakwater' against immorality and unbelief, and on such considerations the probabilities of its restoration to unity will mainly hinge. This is with me no new view. I said in an Anglican publication nine years ago: 'Nor is it unimportant to point

---

* See *Eirenicon*, pp. 282–3: 'Never, I am satisfied, was the work of God among us *so wide and so deep* as now. . . . . The leaven, which was hidden in the meal, has worked secretly, and has now *more centres*, from which it is *everywhere* working.' I believe this is the opinion of all who know most of the facts.

out the duty of seeking rather to win than to repel those who are conscientiously opposed to us (and there are surely conscientious and earnest men still to be found in the Evangelical ranks); not by compromising one iota of the truth, but by presenting it in the form most likely to remove their prejudices, and to commend itself to their serious convictions. What might have been done had such a line been systematically pursued, we may gather from what has resulted even under most unfavourable circumstances. . . . There is much *in the present aspect of parties among us* which gives encouragement for energy and ground for hope. . . Starting from small beginnings, *and increasing with a silent growth*, the Catholic movement has advanced and prospered till, in spite of bitter opposition and many grave discouragements, it seems in a fair way to leaven the general mind of the National Church." *

It has, further, to be borne in mind, that the factors we have to reckon with in dealing with the Church of England, are the High Church, and what is called the Liberal party; and we have many points of contact with both, though more with the former than with the latter. There are those, indeed, on either side, who use a different language, and seem inclined to make 'destruction to the Liberals' the war-cry of a Reunion crusade. Such will not be, and is not, the wish or the policy of the more

---

* Preface to *Church Parties*, 1857, pp. v. viii. ix.

generous spirits in their communion or in ours. The great champion of Catholicism on the Continent has publicly recorded his conviction, that one of the most essential conditions for reuniting our separated brethren, is 'the sincere recognition of goodness and truth, *wherever found*;' and he reminds us that, as Sinbad's magnetic island drew to itself all the iron out of the ship, so it is the Church's office to attract and appropriate as her own all that is good and true in rival systems, since through error we attain to truth, and error only lives by virtue of those germs of truth it really contains, though it misapplies and distorts them.* Dr. Newman says, with that large-minded charity which is characteristic of him, in reference to persons who are perplexed or alienated by the seeming conflict of modern discoveries with traditional belief, 'Who does not feel for such men? who can have one unkind thought of them? I take up St. Augustine's beautiful words: "Illi in vos sæviant," etc. Let those be fierce with you who have no experience of the difficulty with which error is discriminated from truth; and the way of life is found amid the illusions of the world. How many Catholics have in their thoughts followed such men, many of them so good, so true, so noble!'† We may take as the spokesman for Anglicans the Bampton

---

* Döllinger's Speech before the Munich Congress. The whole passage, with some others bearing on reunion, will be found in the Appendix.

† *Apologia pro Vitâ Suâ*, p. 104.

lecturer for this year, who is one of the first preachers in the Established Church, and a leading member of the Catholic party within its pale. He observes, that 'with intellect itself—with the thought of man recognising at once its power and its weakness, its vast range and its necessary limits—religion has, can have, no quarrel. It were a libel on the All-wise Creator to suppose that between intellect and spirit, between thought and faith, there could be any original relations other than those of perfect harmony.'* Nor are the leading organs of the party less outspoken. The 'Christian Remembrancer,' in reviewing a striking sermon of Mr. Cazenove's, on 'Probabilities of Union,' says, not less forcibly than justly, 'It will tend to remove in many minds the growth of a conviction that much of the liberalism of the present day is the cold and negative result of mere indifference in religion. *Such we believe not to be the case*; Liberalism has its better side, and with better minds toleration of each other's views has a direct tendency towards appreciation; *and in mutual appreciation lies the only road to agreement in spirit, and eventually in form.*'† The 'Ecclesiastic' had said already, in reviewing a book of mine, 'We have no panic fear of what is called Liberalism. It is not all evil; and we believe that the right way to meet it is not by proscriptions and anathemas, but by charity and kindly feeling. It is a recoil, a just recoil,

---

* Liddon's *University Sermons*, p. 159.
† *Chr. Rem.*, Jan. 1866, p. 244.

from a narrow system and a base theology; and whether it shall settle in the mean, or go forward to the opposite extreme, will depend very much on the attitude assumed towards it by the Catholic party in the Church of England.'*

For myself, I can never abandon the hope and the conviction that the second great party in the Anglican Church—which has *mutatis mutandis* its representatives among ourselves—will find not only its needful corrective, but a place and a home in a reunited Christendom. The Evangelicals I pass over naturally, because, noble as was their early devotion in an age which had forgotten Christ, and though many admirable and excellent men are still ranged under their banners, while many more have left their ranks for the service of a purer faith, their work has long been done. The party, *as a party*, is too divided and decrepit now to exert any critical influence, and too hopelessly incompetent to deserve it. Dr. Pusey manifests considerable alarm as to the possible obstacles to reunion from an extreme section among ourselves. But when once any scheme of reconciliation is being practically considered, it is hardly likely to be wrecked by the joint anathema of those rival prophets of disunion, the 'Dublin Review' and the 'Record.'

To turn, secondly, to the recent ritual developments of Anglicanism: it seems to me, considering the nature and circumstances of the movement,

---

* *Ecclesiastic*, Aug. 1865, p. 379.

nothing short of paradoxical to regard it as other than a decided advance in a Catholic direction. In itself, of course, ceremonial religion is of very small importance, and the measure of its influence for edification varies indefinitely with different minds. But the contrast between the present 'Ritualists' and those of twenty-five years ago is suggestive in more ways than one. Then, all England was set in a blaze, towns placarded, churches gutted, clergymen mobbed, bishops rebelled against, because it was sought to introduce a few trivial changes, either having no doctrinal significance whatever, or tending (as in the famous crusade for the 'Church Militant Prayer') to obscure rather than to illustrate Catholic belief. Now, in many churches, both in London and elsewhere, all or nearly all the ritual of the Mass has been adopted, not only without protest on the part of the congregations, but with their hearty concurrence, and often at their urgent desire; while in many more churches there is a more or less close approximation to the same ideal of worship. Two large editions have been sold, and a third advertised, of the 'Directorium Anglicanum,' which supplies minute directions for these services drawn from the Sarum Missal. It is, of course, very possible to believe firmly in the Real Presence and the Eucharistic Sacrifice without lighting candles or wearing a chasuble; and I doubt not there are multitudes who do so. What is simply inconceivable is, that men who are neither babies nor buffoons, should care to dress themselves, or see others dressed, in vestments indelibly associated to the popular mind by the immemorial usage of at least fifteen centuries with doctrines which they do not hold themselves. Such incredible folly would be fitter for a strait waistcoat than an alb. The Jesuit reviewer is with me here: 'What marks the difference between the timid reserve of 1840 and the attitude of to-day, is the sight of the ornaments of the Catholic priesthood restored in so many churches; *for these alone express and represent a complete profession of faith in the Eucharistic Sacrifice.**

Neither, indeed, are we left to mere conjectural inference in the matter. There has been, coincidently with the advance in outward ceremonial, and rather heralding than following it, an equally marked advance in the tone of Anglican devotional literature on the Eucharist. Twenty years ago the Bishop of Oxford's 'Eucharistica,' which does not generally rise above devout Zwinglianism, was the favourite High Church manual. Such books as Mr. Orby Shipley's 'Divine Liturgy,' the 'Eucharistic Manual,' the 'Manual of Devotions for the Blessed Sacrament,' lately republished by Mr. F. G. Lee, and Dr. Pusey's translation of the 'Devotions for Communion,' in the *Paradisus*, now in its third edition, are but specimens of many kindred publications, which unmistakably indicate the present belief of

---

* *Etudes Religieuses*, No. 37, pp. 137–8.

Anglicans in the great mystery of the altar; to say nothing of the largely increased number (as I am informed), and more frequent attendance of communicants of both sexes, and of the growing practice of confession. When, therefore, Dr. Pusey, who had already written two learned works in defence of the doctrine of the Real Presence, maintains in the 'Eirenicon' that there is no essential difference on this point between Anglican belief and the Council of Trent, this is no mere isolated expression of individual opinion; it is true, at least, of a large and increasing body of his co-religionists. The Anglican bishops are every year ordaining—and know that they must ordain, whether they like it or not—men who hold this doctrine, and mean to teach it, not wrapped up in a haze of unintelligible shibboleths, but in language their flocks can perfectly comprehend, and are quite prepared to listen to. Candidates for confirmation and first communion are taught it in larger numbers every year, and once taught it is not easily forgotten. The 'Christian Remembrancer,' in the article already referred to (which is commonly attributed to a distinguished Cambridge divine), designates the difference between Roman and Anglican doctrine on the Eucharist as merely 'a philosophical difference of expression which, perhaps, resolves itself into a difference of words,' and is careful to note the importance of discriminating between an objective and subjective Presence, because, in Dr. Pusey's words, 'the doctrine of the Eucharistic Sacrifice depends upon the doctrine of the real objective Presence.' And this doctrine, the reviewer assures us, '*is openly preached in every quarter of the land.*'

If, then, the adoption of Catholic ceremonial implies, as we have seen, the adoption and inculcation of Catholic doctrine, we may naturally ask how such teaching — both on the Eucharist and other points—has been generally received. Our informant replies : 'A traditional interpretation with which the Articles had become encrusted for even three hundred years—an interpretation, too, be it remembered, which was at many points distinctly in contradiction of the express doctrines contained in the Prayer Book of the Church of England—*was, in fact, broken through by Tract* 90. Alas for the cost at which it was done! *But it has been effectually done.*' That is to say, Dr. Newman sowed, in 1841, the harvest which is being reaped in 1866. *Then,* the claim that was tentatively, almost timidly, made by one of the first of living writers, the greatest theologian of his Church, and the man who, more than any of his contemporaries, had stamped the impress of his mind on the religious thought of England, was greeted with a frantic howl of all but unanimous execration from the press, the pulpit, and even the episcopal bench—an outcry as senseless as that of the Ephesian idolators, and in which the courtesies, and even the decencies, of civilised controversy were forgotten. How has the 'Eireni-

con,' which goes beyond Tract 90, and the republication of the Tract itself, which appears as its supplement, been received *now?* I will again quote the ' Remembrancer :' ' What could not be put out then without a storm of abuse following, is received now with acquiescence by one party, and with admiration by another;* whilst the third great party into which we are divided is too feeble to put out any united efforts to destroy what it abominates.' †
The writer adds, still more emphatically, that the review of the 'Eirenicon' which appeared last December in the 'Times,' and was at once hailed as a happy omen by the author and all who sympathise with him, 'attests the fact that the claims which were made twenty-five years ago to hold Roman doctrine have won their way, till at length they are tolerated in the English Church, and are daily making proselytes, *simply because truth is more powerful than error.* . . . The point upon which we now insist is that what was condemned in every quarter of the land in 1841, is held by public opinion to be entirely tenable in 1865, and *is in fact held by nearly all the learned laity and clergy*

---

* I cannot but express my sincere regret that so respectable and influential a newspaper as the *Guardian* should have understood the drift and leading aim of the *Eirenicon*, and of Dr. Newman's letter on it, in a sense which seems to me simply paradoxical.

† This 'total collapse of a great theological bugbear' is admirably drawn out by Dean Stanley in the *Contemporary Review* for April, pp. 544, sqq.

of the Church of England.'* The last words are certainly startling, but the writer can judge better than we can the state of feeling in his own communion.

It will of course be objected by some that, after all, the wide divergences of opinion among Anglicans are too great to offer any reasonable hope of religious unity. As regards the Liberals, I have said something already. We have the unhesitating testimony of a clear-sighted and influential Anglican writer, that ' the " Evangelical " clergy, on the whole, are steadily advancing towards a higher measure of truth than they had attained in past years;' and, where they do not sink into Rationalism, are 'perpetually rising' towards Catholic belief.† And I would reply, more generally, with the Jesuit reviewer in the ' Études Religieuses,' that such divergences are the inevitable result of a state of ecclesiastical isolation, and can only be estimated fairly if we place ourselves in the position of the Anglicans (no difficult task, anyhow, for those who know it by experience). He adds very justly, and in the sense of a striking passage in your own

---

* I do not think the *Christian Remembrancer* does at all overestimate the significance, as a moral fact, of this review in the *Times*, which seldom notices theological works at all—whether we consider the place it appeared in, or its general character and reputed authorship, or its conciliatory method of handling the question, or its marked tone of deferential courtesy towards the author of the *Eirenicon*.

† See Sermon signed ' L.,' in Second Series of *Sermons on Reunion*, pp. 158–59.

review, 'Does any one suppose there was no diversity of opinion among the Donatists before they were reunited to the Church at the Council of Carthage? What endless negotiations were found necessary, at the Council of Florence, for arranging the union between Greeks and Latins; and what variety of views displayed itself among the Greeks! And so it was at the Council of Brecz, when the Russian bishops resolved to return to unity.' *

And now it is time to speak more directly of the work which has suggested these preliminary observations. I quite agree with our excellent friend, Mr. de Lisle, who has perhaps done more than any man living to merit the Beatitude pronounced on the peacemakers, 'that its publication marks an epoch in the ecclesiastical history of the nineteenth century, and that it is the first grand step towards a *corporate and organic* healing of the deplorable divisions in the Christian family;' † and that, not only from the way it has been generally received, which I have already dwelt upon, but because, in Dr. Newman's words, it has 'put the whole argument' between Anglicans and ourselves 'on a new footing.' It does so first, by the friendly and conciliatory spirit in which the writer approaches us, and his evident *desire* to discover a basis of agreement rather than matter of difference; and in this respect it is, to use your own words, 'a wonderful advance on the usual

---

* *Études Rel.* No. 38, pp. 268–70.
† See his communicated article in *Union Review* for Jan. 1866.

forms of Protestant controversy,' and may indeed be taken as a response on the Anglican side to an interesting and able Catholic work, which attracted considerable attention last year, by a common friend of ours, now, as formerly at Oxford.* It does so, secondly, by the *method* of treating our differences which it both indicates and largely exemplifies, and which cannot but have a far wider application than to any particular formula, such as the 39 Articles, or any single doctrine, however important, such as that of Justification.† I mean the method of *explaining*, already suggested as regards the Articles by Tract 90, as previously on our side by Sancta Clara, but never before so emphatically put forward from an influential quarter in the Church of England, in the sense of a *direct challenge to reunion on the doctrinal basis of the Council of Trent*. That this is the main drift and purpose of Dr. Pusey's book must have been evident to every attentive reader from the first, and you had accordingly so construed it yourself. But we need not rely on inferences however demonstrable, for the author has become his own interpreter in a letter to the 'Weekly Register' of Nov. 25, occasioned by your review. He there says, 'I am thankful that you have brought out the main drift and object of my "Eirenicon," what, in my mind,

---

* Ffoulkes' *Christendom's Divisions*, of which a second volume is advertised to appear in June.

† Indeed, on 'Original Sin, Justification, and the doctrines of Grace,' Dr. Pusey thinks no explanations are needed.

underlies the whole, to show that, *in my conviction, there is no insurmountable obstacle to the union of the Roman, Greek, and Anglican communions.** I have long been convinced that there is nothing in the Council of Trent which could not be explained satisfactorily to us, if it were explained authoritatively; . . . . nothing in our Articles which cannot be explained rightly, as not contradicting anything held to be *de fide* in the Roman Church. The great body of the faith is held alike by both.' And he repeats, in a letter to the 'John Bull,' of Dec. 9, that ' the Council of Trent is not an insurmountable obstacle to reunion,' nor the 'primacy of the Bishop of Rome' either. It would be hard to exaggerate the significance of such a statement, publicly made in the face of England and of Christendom, by one whose influence Dr. Newman considers—rightly, I suppose —to be greater than that of any single individual in his own communion, in the Greek Church, or among ourselves. To the particular case of the 39 Articles I shall have occasion to revert, in another connection, later; but Dr. Pusey's suggestion for removing their difficulties by explanation contains, as was implied just now, a great principle, so momentous in its bearing on the whole subject, that it must not be passed over in silence here.

Let me begin by observing that the same principle was laid down for our guidance also twenty-five years ago in words which can hardly be too often or

* The italics are the writer's.

too emphatically repeated, by a high authority among ourselves. '*We must explain to the utmost.*'* This is no mere appropriate act of courtesy or graceful concession to the requirements of controversial etiquette. It is a sacred duty which we owe to our separated countrymen and to the majesty of truth, not to allow them, through any negligence on our part, to misunderstand language expressive of Catholic doctrine to which they have often learnt, om accident or from the bitterness of past religious feuds, to attach a meaning ' clean from the purpose of the things themselves.' Such theological terms, for instance, as ' merit,' ' penance,' 'satisfaction,' 'supererogation,' and others that might be named, are to many Protestants suggestive of ideas which we should be the first to repudiate. And as examples of what I mean by explaining, I may be allowed to refer first to a work I have elsewhere had occasion to commend to the notice of Anglicans,† Bishop Ullathorne's ' Immaculate Conception,' which quite removed from my own mind, when an Anglican, the historical and doctrinal difficulties surrounding the question. So, again, I may point to the note appended to Canon Oakeley's recent letter to the Archbishop, on the terms ' worship,' ' veneration,' and the like, as applied to the *cultus* of the Blessed Virgin and the Saints.‡ And

---

* Cardinal Wiseman's *Letter to Lord Shrewsbury*, p. 31. You have similarly urged the importance of ' a disposition on our side *to explain, and to receive explanations*, in a conciliatory spirit.' —*Review*, p. 17.

† *Catholic Doctrine of Atonement*, Note to Introduction, p. li.

‡ At the same time it seems to me better in every way to keep

a still more conspicuous illustration may be found in Dr. Newman's luminous exposition of the doctrines

to the language of the Council of Trent, which speaks, as does Pius IV's Creed, of 'honouring' and 'invoking' the Saints, and to avoid using the English word 'adoration' in that sense, though it is no doubt, as Canon Oakeley justly observes, quite defensible and etymologically correct, meaning in fact no more than 'praying to.' And accordingly the Latin term 'adorare' is excused, though not insisted on, by the Tridentine Catechism, in this limited sense. But the etymological sense of a word and its common acceptance do not always coincide, and we must use words as others use them, if we do not want to be misunderstood. 'Honour,' 'reverence,' 'veneration,' which are the words used in Cardinal Wiseman's Sermons, are not reasonably open to misconstruction, but in ordinary use 'adoration' has come to be the nearest English equivalent to the theological term '*latria*,' i.e. the supreme homage due from the creature to the Creator. Of course no Catholic dreams of applying it in this sense to our Lady. But if we do apply it to her, we must reckon on being almost inevitably misunderstood by the majority of our countrymen. And moreover, the traditional feeling and language of English Catholics bears me out in this. In *Roman Catholic Principles* (London 1865), first published in 1680, and frequently republished since under high ecclesiastical and episcopal sanction, we find (p. 15): 'God alone we *worship and adore*,' while of devotion to the Saints it is said, ' Can this manner of *invocation* be more injurious to Christ our *Mediator* than it is for one Christian to beg the prayers of another here on earth'?[1] Bishop Milner, in his *End of Controversy*, cites from 'a work of great authority among Catholics, first published by our eminent divine Gother, and republished by our venerable Bishop Challoner,' the following anathema: 'Cursed be every goddess-worshipper; that believes the Blessed Virgin to be any more than a creature; that *worships* her, or puts his trust in her more than in God; that believes her above her Son, or that she can in anything command Him.' Accordingly, in the *First Catechism of Christian Doctrine*, which is 'approved for the use of the faithful

---

[1] The italics here are in the original.

of Original Sin and the Immaculate Conception in his Letter on the 'Eirenicon.' If it is not an impertinence to introduce what is so noble a poem, though it is also much more than poetry, in something like a controversial connection, I would add that the same illustrious author's 'Dream of Gerontius' will to many readers throw quite a new light on the Catholic doctrine of Purgatory, which they may perhaps have learnt to regard with an ill-defined dislike, based on misconceptions.* Indeed there is a passage in Dr. Pusey's book (pp. 191–92) which sounds almost like an echo of some of the most striking lines in the Poem, where he says, 'On our side, to thoughtful minds, whom the grace of God has taught something of what sin is, and of the holiness and love of God and of Jesus, it is absolutely inconceivable that,— when the soul shall first behold Jesus, and in His sight, with its powers quickened by Him, shall be-

in all the dioceses of England and Wales,' the word '*adored*' is used in explaining the first commandment (p. 24) as equivalent to 'honoured *as gods*,' and this 'supreme or divine honour' is next distinguished from the 'inferior honour' given to the Saints; and therefore, in the forms both of Morning and Evening Prayer at the end of the Catechism, 'I *adore* Thee' occurs as an act of homage to Almighty God; but the word is nowhere applied to the Saints. So, again, in our authorised translation of the Nicene Creed, 'who together with the Father and the Son is *adored* and glorified.' And the word is in like manner exclusively reserved for the worship of Almighty God or the Persons of the Holy Trinity in the authorised translation of the *Raccolta* by F. St. John of the Birmingham Oratory.

* Since the above was written, an appreciative review of the poem has appeared in the *Spectator* for March 3.

hold its past life, as a whole;... *it should not have intense pain*, pain so intense, that one should think that, in this life, soul and body would be severed by its intensity.' How does this differ from Dr. Newman's description of the parted soul flying 'with the intemperate energy of love' to the feet of Jesus?

> But, ere it reach them, the keen sanctity,
> Which with its effluence, like a glory, clothes
> And circles round the Crucified, has seized,
> *And scorched, and shrivelled it*; and now it lies
> Passive and still before the awful Throne.
> *O happy, suffering* soul ! for it is safe,
> *Consumed, yet quickened, by the glance of God.**

It has been acutely observed that half the disputes in the world arise from using terms in different senses. Dr. Döllinger goes further, in reference to religious controversies, when he says that four-fifths of the Protestant objections to Catholicism either relate to what is accidental or are mere logomachies.† And his remark had been anticipated by the late Bishop Doyle in his letter to Lord Ripon, published in 1824, where he first enumerates all the principal points at issue between the rival creeds, and then adds, 'On most of these it appears to me there is *no essential*

---

* *Dream of Gerontius*, pp. 50–51. There is evidently a growing tendency among both Anglican and Lutheran divines to recognise the reasonableness of some doctrine of Purgatory. Instances of this, as regards the latter, will be found in my *Catholic Doctrine of the Atonement*, pp. 179, 181.

† *The Church and the Churches*, p. 16 (Mac Cabe's translation).

difference between Catholics and Protestants; the existing diversity of opinion arises, in most cases, from certain *forms of words,* which admit of satisfactory explanation, or from the ignorance or misconceptions which ancient prejudice and ill-will produce, but which could be removed.'*

As regards the special case of Anglicanism, we have also the emphatic testimony to the same effect of the late illustrious primates of the Catholic Church in England and Ireland. Cardinal Wiseman speaks of Tract 90 as supplying 'the demonstration that such interpretation may be given to the most difficult [of the 39] Articles as will strip them of all contradiction to the decrees of the Tridentine Synod.' † And Archbishop Murray, commenting on his Suffragan's Letter to Lord Ripon, quoted above, observes that, 'were Church of England people true to the principles laid down in their Prayer Book, the doctrinal differences which *appear* considerable, *but are not,* would soon be removed.' ‡ I well remember the surprise of an excellent and talented 'Evangelical' clergyman, a friend and old

---

* *Life, Times, and Correspondence of Dr. Doyle,* by W. J. Fitzpatrick, vol. i. p. 423. In the same letter he expresses his willingness to resign his bishopric 'most cheerfully, and without fee, pension, emolument, or hope,' if he could thereby contribute to 'the union of the Churches;' adding his conviction that the Irish Catholic clergy 'would, without an exception, make every possible sacrifice to effect a union.'

† *Letter to Lord Shrewsbury,* p. 38.

‡ MS. Letter to Æneas Macdonnell. The original has been kindly shown me by its present possessor.

schoolfellow of my own, on my assuring him that the necessity of Divine grace for pleasing God was recognised, or rather insisted on, by Catholics. He had thought our doctrine of merit meant Pelagianism. Nor should it be forgotten that mutual explanations would clear up many objections to supposed doctrines which, at best, are no more than pious or probable opinions. Dr. Döllinger reminds us that 'the Schoolmen considered it no less a heresy to call that *de fide* which is not, than to deny that which is.' *

I cannot better conclude these remarks on the duty of explaining, with a view to mutual agreement, than in the words of the important document I began by quoting, and which, alike from its authorship and its contents, has, as you have yourself pointed out, a prominent claim on the attention of all who are interested in the sacred cause of reunion: 'I have thus indirectly stated what would seem to be our first duty; to offer cheerfully and honestly every explanation in our power, and point out where our real doctrines are mistaken, where they are confounded with mere permissive practices, and where they may be liable to abuse. The sooner a clear and distinct understanding can be come to upon these matters, whether by personal conference or by writing, the better for the cause. There exist at this moment, I am sure, grievous misapprehensions in the minds of serious men connected with the new

* Speech at close of Munich Congress.

movement, upon this point, which it seems to me a more direct and friendly intercourse, directed to this purpose, could remove.'*

And here, after speaking of the duty of mutual explanations, seems to be the natural place for pointing out a serious mistake into which Dr. Pusey (in common, I suspect, with the great majority of Anglicans) has fallen, but which I am sure he will be glad to have corrected; and what appears to me an entire misconception of *his* meaning by one of his Catholic critics, whose name and position will give to his words an influence he certainly would not desire them to exert in a sense likely to mislead.

In referring to the Sacrament of Extreme Unction, which he is very laudably desirous to see restored in his own communion, Dr. Pusey dwells at great length on a distinction between the practice of the ancient, as still of the Eastern, Church—where restoration of bodily health is recognised as one end of the sacrament—and that which he ascribes to us, of administering it 'only when, in man's sight, such restoration is impossible.' He considers this to be 'the corrupt following of the Apostles,' censured in Article XXII., and implies, if I understand him rightly, that we have departed as far from apostolical precedent, in excluding, or omitting, from our use of the Sacrament the notion of bodily cure, as the Church of England in dropping the use of it alto-

---

* *Letter to Lord Shrewsbury*, p. 33.

gether.* Now, even if the charge brought against us were correct, it would not amount to very much. It is by no means self-evident, as Dr. Pusey assumes, that St. James's words refer at all to bodily healing.† Both σώσει and ἐγερεῖ may have a purely spiritual application. And, supposing either or both of the words do refer to bodily recovery—as the latter very probably does, at least inclusively—it would not follow that such results were to be looked for now. The Apostolic Church was instinct with supernatural powers; it lived and moved and had its being in an atmosphere of miracle. Not only were sacraments, especially Confirmation, the ordinary channels of extraordinary gifts, but its least benediction—the touch of consecrated hands, or of handkerchiefs they had touched, or the passing shadow of an Apostle—were instruments of healing, as, on the other hand, the profanation of sacraments was punished with disease or death.‡ All this has passed away; but Dr. Pusey would not consider the Sacrament of Confirmation, which his Church retains, 'a corrupt following of the Apostles,' because it is no longe accompanied, as in their day, by the gift of tongues, or by prayer for it. Why, then, should not the Sacrament of Unction be retained, though all notion of miraculous cure (and any cure so wrought must be of a miraculous kind) had been given up?

However, the fact is that Dr. Pusey is quite mis-

---

* See *Eirenicon*, pp. 219-228. † James v. 15.
‡ Acts viii. 18; xix. 6, 12; 1 Cor. xi. 30.

taken about our usage. And I cannot but feel some surprise that so learned a writer, after quoting prayers for bodily healing from the form of administering unction in the Greek 'Euchologion' and the First Prayer Book of Edward VI., should have omitted to look at the Roman Ritual, from which he assumes such prayers to be omitted. A very cursory glance would have convinced him of his mistake. Not only do the Rubrics expressly forbid the administration of the Sacrament, *where restoration of bodily health is out of the question*, and for that reason, as the Tridentine Catechism teaches—as, e. g. to those under sentence of execution, or in danger of shipwreck, or of dying in battle—and describe it as 'cœlestis medicina non animæ solum, sed etiam corpori salutaris;' but of the three Collects used in the Ritual, the first and longest is equally divided between prayer for bodily and spiritual assistance, and the third is exclusively occupied with restoration of bodily strength. There is no contrast whatever in this respect between the Greek Ritual or the first Reformed Prayer Book, which Dr. Pusey quotes, and the Roman. For our formal teaching, the Council of Trent declares its last effect to be 'sanitatem corporis interdum, ubi saluti animæ expedierit,' and only anathematises those who maintain this to have been its *sole* end, and that it has therefore now ceased.* The Catechism of Trent is more explicit still. It

---

* Sep. xiv. cap. 2, and can. 2 *De Extr. Unct.*

declares the Sacrament to be ordained 'not only to supply medicine for the soul, but for the body too,' though '*rather* for soul than body;' and that the reason it operates so seldom now for bodily health is from the feeble faith of those who receive or administer it.* And in accordance with this teaching of formal documents, our popular manual of instruction, the 'First Catechism of Christian Doctrine,' has the following Question and Answer (p. 37): 'What are the effects of this Sacrament?' (i.e Unction.) 'It comforts the soul in her last agony, it remits sin, and also restores health, *when God sees it to be expedient.*' And as regards our practice; so far is it from being usual 'not to anoint the sick until they are "in extremis,"' that I well remember Dr. Weathers, the present excellent President of St. Edmund's College, Herts (the Theological Seminary of this diocese), distinctly cautioning us, in a moral theology lecture, *to be on our guard against* a popular superstition among the poor, who often shrink from receiving this sacrament till the last moment, from an ignorant notion that receiving it implies they are about to die.† If my memory does

---

* See *Cat. Conc. Trid.*, pars ii. cap. 13, 16, 17, 19, 28, 29.

† A priest of considerable experience in Ireland assures me that *there* a precisely opposite danger has to be guarded against. So strong is the popular belief in the *healing* power of the Sacrament, that it is constantly asked for as a remedy in what cannot be considered cases of serious illness at all. And popular belief in Ireland is more likely to exaggerate Catholic tradition than to run counter to it.

not deceive me, the Anglican clergy often have a precisely similar difficulty to contend with about the Eucharist, which the poor of their flock are very apt to regard in like manner as a kind of death-warrant.

Dr. Pusey starts a further difficulty as to how Extreme Unction can be said to remit sin, or 'the remains of sin,' when it has been already remitted by absolution. It might be enough to reply, that the difficulty applies quite as much to St. James's words as to those of the Council of Trent; for, whether or not we understand the Apostle to connect bodily cure with the Sacrament, there can be no doubt whatever that he connects remission of sin with it. But, moreover, the argument would prove too much. Venial sin does not require absolution, and mortal sin is forgiven at once through an act of perfect contrition. Yet a very large moiety of the sins confessed sacramentally are either venial or (one would hope) have already been put away by an act of sincere contrition; and I think Dr. Pusey would agree with us in wishing them to be confessed notwithstanding. So too in the Anglican, as in the Roman, Ritual, a general absolution is pronounced over communicants before they receive the Eucharist; yet in either case they may have just before been separately absolved. Does not the whole difficulty find its practical solution in the words of the 'Miserere' Psalm, '*Amplius* lava me ab iniquitate meâ,' 'Wash me *more and more*' (or, as the Anglican Psalter renders it, 'wash me *throughly*') 'from my iniquity?' And the wise man bids us 'not be without fear of *forgiven* sin.'* I recollect a very beautiful passage on this subject which occurs somewhere in Faber's 'Growth in Holiness;' and an ancient prayer, which Dr. Pusey quotes in his edition of Jeremy Taylor's 'Golden Grove,' is to the same effect, 'Da *semper dolere*, et de dolere gaudere.'

And now I turn for a moment to what appears to me, speaking with great diffidence, a grave misconception of Dr. Pusey's meaning on an important point into which Canon Oakeley has fallen at the close of his eloquent Letter to the Archbishop on the Leading Topics of the 'Eirenicon.' Dr. Pusey quotes in his first letter to the 'Weekly Register,' the saying of 'a very eminent Italian nobleman,' to the effect that 'your (Anglican) *maximum* and our (Catholic) *minimum* might be found to harmonise.' The expression is scarcely a happy one; but judging from the context, I should certainly have supposed Dr. Pusey to mean no more than this: that the belief of a consistent Anglican would not fall short of what is required as 'de fide' by the Roman Church. And so understood, the statement is at least innocuous. Canon Oakeley, however, understands it very differently. He draws out, with that force and elegance of diction which always makes it an intellectual treat to read what he has written, whether one agrees with it or not, his idea of the *character* of a '*minimum* Catholic,' not of the minimum of

---

* Ecclus. v. 5.

doctrinal belief required by the Catholic Church. And he includes in his picture some matters of mere personal feeling or variable opinion, on which equally good Catholics may and do differ from one another, some habits of mind which are simply marks of an *irreligious* man, to whatever communion he may belong, and some ideas which may be loosely entertained by some half-believing Christians of very confused intellect, but can only be logically adopted by an atheist. He then proceeds to ask whether it is to effect such a result 'that Dr. Pusey would employ the latest energies of a life, laboriously and honourably spent in the inculcation and exemplification of principles the very reverse of those on which such a character is founded?' Surely the question answers itself. I cannot but think that, on examining more closely the passage in Dr. Pusey's letter, which he was commenting on, his distinguished critic will be prepared to confess that he has unwittingly but completely misinterpreted it. And I feel confident, if only from the graceful and ungrudging tribute to Dr. Pusey with which his own Letter commences, that no one would be more rejoiced than himself to find that such was the case.

Will Canon Oakeley forgive me if, before quitting his Letter, I venture one more criticism on an earlier passage in it, where he also appears to me—though I speak with more hesitation in this case—to have given to Dr. Pusey's words a sense which they need not, and I would fain hope do not, bear. He does not specify the passages to which he refers, but he tells us that certain portions of the 'Eirenicon' make him suspect its author of desiring to apply 'the principle of finality' to the dogmatic utterances of the Church. No one can suspect me of any sympathy with an idea which I have explicitly denounced in a recent work, and in language (if it is not presumptuous in me to say so) closely akin to that employed here by Canon Oakeley.* I most entirely agree with him that such a theory is subversive of the very notion of the Church as 'a visible institution, ruled habitually by the Holy Ghost.' It is also subversive of the principle of development, without which, as Dr. Newman has lately reminded us in his Letter on the 'Eirenicon,' it would be very hard to defend the doctrines of the Trinity and Incarnation, and other fundamental Christian verities. But I am not at all clear that Dr. Pusey would deny this in principle, though he might differ from us about its application. What I conceive him to be protesting against is, first, the right of what he, as an Anglican, considers a part only of the Church to speak in the name of the whole;† secondly, and still more, certain modern opinions about the nature and exercise of infallibility, which he has chiefly gathered from some recent articles in the 'Dublin Review,' and of which

* See *Catholic Doctrine of Atonement*, Introduction, pp. xvii. xviii.

† *Eirenicon*, pp. 83, 84.

I shall merely observe here, that to a very large number of Catholics they will appear quite as wildly extravagant as they possibly can to Dr. Pusey. But I do not understand him to deny the right and office of the Church to define her doctrine, from time to time, as need arises, under the divine guidance of the Holy Ghost. However, I speak under correction; and, as two forthcoming works of the author, in defence of his 'Eirenicon,' are advertised, we shall probably be better able to fix his precise meaning before long than we are now. On the subject of development I shall have something to say further on.

I am not writing a review of the 'Eirenicon,' but simply considering it in relation to Catholic unity. There is no need, therefore, for any detailed examination here of that portion of the work—considerable in extent, but inconsiderable in importance, as compared with its main drift and professed object—which deals with what the author regards as prevalent and popular exaggerations of Catholic belief or practice, chiefly on two points—devotion to our Lady, and the infallibility of the Pope. The first has already been handled by one to whom it is a truism rather than a compliment to apply the Ciceronian dictum, 'Nihil tetigit quod non ornavit,' and handled in a way which makes further comment at once an impertinence and a mistake. And Dr. Newman's letter contains a distinct intimation (p. 18) of his intending to take up the other question also. What

I desire to insist upon here is the singular unanimity, in one very important respect, of the reply which has been made to this part of Dr. Pusey's indictment.* Some critics indeed have (most unfortunately, as it appears to me) written as though they meant to accuse him of intentional unfairness or dishonesty—a charge which none who know anything of him could for a moment tolerate. But the very fact of their urging it implies their agreement with those who have pointed out, in a juster and more kindly spirit, that the strange views or devotions he excepts against, and which he seems unwillingly disposed to regard as expressing a dominant 'system' in the Church, are but the extreme and unauthorised idiosyncracies of individuals. You, my dear Father Lockhart, in your interesting review of the 'Eirenicon,' were the first to call attention to this, and to assure the author that he need have no fear of what he, not unreasonably, shrinks from, as inconsistent with reason and right devotion, being forced either on individuals or communities on their reconciliation with the Holy See. Dr. Newman went a good deal further. He not only said, 'If the Catholic faith spreads in England, *these peculiarities will not spread*

* The only exception I have come across is a feeble and indecorous attack on Dr. Newman by an obscure correspondent of the *Tablet*, with whom the editor, as might have been expected, had the good sense and good feeling to disclaim any sympathy. (This note was written before the Bishop of Clifton's dignified rebuke of this ' intemperate writer ' had given his lordship a fresh claim on the gratitude of English Catholics.)

with it;' but he proceeded to collect into two pages of masterly analysis the substance of all the most offensive passages quoted in Dr. Pusey's book, and expended two pages more of that language in which few, if any, can rival him, and which once read fixes itself indelibly on the memory, in recording his indignant repudiation of statements which ' defy all the *loci theologici,* and can only be explained by being explained away.' * The editor of the (Jesuit) ' Études Religieuses ' endorses his repudiation of this '*pretended* popular system,' and adds that, since Bourdaloue's Sermon on the subject, there has been no more luminous exposition of the difference between true and false devotion to Mary. And the reviewer of the ' Eirenicon' in that journal, while declining to inquire into the authorship of the extraordinary passages quoted in it, insists that ' very few Catholics ever heard of them ;' but that in matters lying beyond the range of fixed dogma the faithful are allowed ' a great liberty,' in accordance with St. Augustine's maxim (which by the way is not his, though it deserves to be), ' In necessariis unitas, in dubiis libertas, in omnibus caritas,' and that the conditions are strictly limited and not often realised, under which alone, even on ' ultramontane ' principles, a papal decree is regarded as infallible.† Canon

---

* The *Saturday Review,* March 24, remarks with honourable candour, on Dr. Newman's Letter : ' Dr. Newman, we need hardly say, writes as what he is and ever will be—*an Englishman, in thought and feeling and education, to the backbone.*'

† *Études Relig.,* No. 37, p. 143 ; No. 38, pp. 274, 283, 288.

Oakeley is less emphatic in his disclaimer of excessive theories, but he also protests against the language of unauthoritative, and perhaps objectionable, writers being taken to represent the teaching of the Church. This leads me to say a few words on the two sources almost exclusively relied on by Dr. Pusey for his unfavourable estimate of the current belief of English Catholics, viz. the works of the late Dr. Faber, and the last few numbers of the ' Dublin Review.' *

As regards the ' Dublin'—not to dwell on its own explicit, though somewhat tardy, admission, that it 'is now a purely private and unofficial periodical,'† or Dr. Newman's assertion that it can '*in no sense*' be understood to speak for English Catholics—it is obvious to remark, what must strike the most casual reader of that periodical, that it bears throughout the unmistakable impress of a mind not only single but singular to an extent which borders on the unique. Of Dr. Faber's writings I should be the last to speak with disrespect, feeling as I do, amid whatever occasional disagreement, how much I owe to them, and still more to the kindness of their gifted and gentle-hearted author, whom to know was to admire and to love. Dr. Faber is indeed 'a popular writer,' and most deservedly so; though I have met with many Catholics, both converts and others, who do not like his writings. They have circulated, however, very widely

---

* A third English writer, Oswald, from whom some shocking passages are quoted, appears to be on the Index.

† *Dublin Review*, Jan. 1866, p. 192.

among Protestants as well as Catholics, and even among Dissenters and Presbyterians.* Scarcely a collection of Hymns for use in the Church of England has appeared for years without containing some of his, nor did he ever refuse to sanction this use of them, when asked, as he himself told me. Some have already become as familiar to the ears and as dear to the hearts of even the most Protestant congregations as 'Rock of Ages' or Ken's Evening Hymn. It is not wonderful that such a writer should be popular with those who know him only by his writings; it would be very wonderful if he were not with those who knew him personally. But his admirers would be the last to forget that among his many gifts and graces not the least conspicuous was the grace of poetry. And this, while it gave to his style an exquisite charm and refinement, and added not a little to the pathos of that winning earnestness which none who ever had the privilege of hearing him preach will easily forget, might surely suggest a caution against pressing with too rigid and literal an exactness the devotional language of one who never lets us forget that he is a poet as well as a divine. I have no intention of defending, as I certainly could not adopt,

* One of the most popular Anglican religious books of the day, which has run through five editions, and lies on every drawingroom table—Dr. Goulburn's *Thoughts on Personal Religion*—is derived, both in detail and in general plan, from one of Faber's most valuable books, *Growth in Holiness*, to an extent which makes one feel surprised that a writer who can so well afford to own his literary obligations should, in this instance, have omitted to do so.

everything he has said about the Blessed Virgin; but there are few writers to whom Dr. Newman's remark applies with more peculiar force: 'When you read anything extravagant in praise of our Lady, is it not charitable to ask, even while you condemn it in itself, *Did the author write nothing else? Did he write on the Blessed Sacrament?* had he given up "*all for Jesus?*"' Faber wrote, as a Catholic, some nine goodly volumes —one being on 'The Blessed Sacrament,' another on doing 'all for Jesus'—which contain throughout, whatever else they may contain also, most abundant and unmistakable evidence of an intense, nay passionate, devotion to our Blessed Lord; but nearly all Dr. Pusey's extracts are taken from a Preface of scarcely as many pages to his translation of a little French Manual, written shortly before his death, and under pressure of severe and painful illness. Dr. Pusey is quite incapable of intentional unfairness, but anyone whose notions of Faber were exclusively derived from the quotations in the 'Eirenicon,' would have about as accurate an impression of his writings, as a whole, as might be gained of Wordsworth's poetry from the 'Rejected Addresses.' There are probably multitudes of his Catholic readers who, like myself, will have obtained their first knowledge of Grignon de Montfort's book, and Faber's Preface to it, from those extracts.* I see,

---

* We claim, after all, no more for our Lady than the great Anglican poet who has just passed to his rest :—

> Ave Maria! Thou whose name
> *All but adoring* love may claim.

Anglicans should not quarrel with us if we are not content with less. Cf. note, p. 23, supra.

from a paper of our friend Mr. de Lisle's, that the late General of your Order, Father Pagani—who was himself a very popular devotional writer, and wrote a great deal about our Lady—considered the language of the book itself (the Preface had not then appeared) 'both mischievous and heretical,'*—not of course meaning that it was so *in the sense intended by the author.* Neither indeed does Dr. Pusey ; for he says, in a letter to the 'Weekly Register,' that he 'was intent only on describing the system he felt to be the great obstacle to Reunion, and had not the least thought of criticising holy men who hold it,' still less of implying ' that they took from our Lord any of the love which they gave to His Mother ;' and in a second letter he more than disarms all hostile criticism by reminding us that his only ground for commenting at all on our practices and beliefs, is his desire to be at one with us. ' In the view of a hoped-for reunion *everything which you do affects us.*'

The following beautiful passage from one of the first Italian theologians of the present century will have, I know, a special authority with you, as coming from the founder and model of your own Institute of Charity. It will at least help to satisfy Dr. Pusey that spiritual writers among us are fully alive to the possible dangers arising from an exaggeration or misuse of devotions lawful and often edifying in themselves, and do not yield to him in

* *Union Review*, Jan. 1866, p. 88.

sensitiveness about what 'even *seems* to interfere with exclusive trust and reliance on Jesus.' And there can, of course, be no thought of a politic or unwilling concession to English prejudices in a work written solely for Italians :—

> Christians have, it is true, particular devotions—practices in honour of the Saints, or of special objects of piety. These are laudable, if approved by the Church; but who can deny that, not through any defect in the devotions themselves, but often through the imperfection of those who use them,* many souls are wholly taken up with them, and thereby, as it were, hindered and kept back from the Fount of all Devotion—from the knowledge and intimate friendship of Jesus, to whose honour all such devotions should be referred? How excellent, how profitable it is to think always on Jesus; and, after the apostolic pattern, to fix our mind on Him in all things! And this, not only remembering that He is God—for the thought of His Godhead alone would but dishearten and confound us—but thinking of Him as Man, as one of ourselves, as clothed with a body like ours, a Man truly subject to human infirmity but without sin, who rejoices and suffers with us, pities and consoles us; cheers, encourages, helps, reproves, and corrects us; who is faithful to us in all things, a Friend in all, ever present, our Intimate and our Companion.†

---

* Dr. Newman insists on the same obvious fact : '*A people's religion is ever a corrupt religion*; . . . if you make use of religion to improve them, they will make use of religion to corrupt it.'— *Letter to Pusey*, p. 86. And all experience proves it.

† *Della Educazione Cristiana*, pp. 133, 134. As an impression has got about in some quarters that Rosmini's works are on the Index, which has been encouraged by the intemperate attack of an ill-informed writer in the *Dublin Review* for Jan. 1866, it may be well to state that two short tracts only of his were placed on the Index—the *Cinque Piaghi* and the *Projetto di una Constituzione*—and those not on theological but political grounds; for they had been originally published with the warm personal

Before quitting this part of the subject, it may be well to lay down one fundamental distinction, which has its bearing on a very large portion of Dr. Pusey's book. And I will do so in words weightier than my own, as coming from one who has been for some forty years a zealous and devoted member of the English Catholic body, and whose 'praise is in all the Churches' for his manifold and munificent deeds of charity. His statement more than counterbalances the strange assertions much dwelt upon in the 'Eirenicon,' but gathered almost exclusively from a few recent articles in one Review, which is the organ of an extreme party among us, and, I strongly suspect, from one writer in it, who is probably the extremest of them all, according to whose opinions, as Dr. Pusey not unreasonably points out, we should be receiving 'almost yearly' additions to the Catholic faith, many of them bearing on purely historical questions.* In most emphatic contradiction to these startling eccentricities of a clique of anonymous dogmatists whom Dr. Pusey has been disposed 'to rest on as authorities,' is the following clear and manly statement of genuine Catholic principles in Mr. de Lisle's 'Remarks on Newman's Letter to Jelf,' published with his name in 1841, and approval of the Holy Father. The rest of his voluminous works (from one of which my extract is taken) were not only not condemned, but were expressly exempted from all censure after a long and rigorous scrutiny.

* The articles referred to not only imply this, as stated at p. 290 of the *Eirenicon,* and claim for every document emanating from

received without one syllable of censure or remonstrance by both the hierarchy and the laity of the Church. The italics are in the original :—

> Neither the Church of Rome, nor the Churches in communion with her, which, taken in their totality, form the Church Catholic, acknowledge *any other authoritative standard of teaching* than the *Council of Trent* and *the other general Councils* which preceded the Tridentine. But I go further; I hesitate not to declare that neither in the *Roman Schools*, to which Mr. Newman appeals as bearing him out in the justice of his distinction, nor *in those* of any other Catholic university, is there *in point of fact* any teaching considered as *authoritative*, whether moral or dogmatical, in any way contrary to or beyond *the Council of Trent*. In asserting this, I do not mean to deny that there are theological *opinions*, left as open questions in the Church, in regard to which Catholic divines are at liberty to follow each his own private judgment, or that *in some particular schools*, in regard to some one or other of these, there may be a general agreement of theologians, and, consequently, a general teaching on the part of the same; but I do most distinctly deny that any such agreement is anything beyond an agreement in *opinion*, or that it could raise any such opinion to the rank of an article of faith, or justify any man in pronouncing it to constitute *the authoritative teaching* of the Roman Catholic Church.*

So far I had written before the distinction Mr. de Lisle is here insisting upon had been so remarkably endorsed by the high sanction of the Bishop of

the Holy See ' an infallibility *equal in extent* to that of the Divine Scriptures' (id. p. 303); but they claim *more*. They imply that every passing and incidental expression in such documents is *verbally inspired*, which is beyond what the great majority of Catholic theologians would maintain of Holy Scripture itself in the present day. Yet this is necessary for the writer's argument; to deny *this* is to deny 'the divine origin of Christianity'!!

* *Remarks on Letter to Jelf*, by A. L. Phillipps, 1841.

Clifton, in his grave and dignified rebuke of a class of writers, who measure their loyalty to the Church by their hatred of their country, and whose standard of common sense is one 'scarcely to be expected of a grown-up man when reasoning on serious subjects.' His lordship will not, I trust, think that I am taking an undue liberty, if I venture to transfer to my pages the concluding paragraphs of his Letter, primarily designed as a check upon intemperate dogmatists among ourselves, but none the less calculated to reassure those who, like Dr. Pusey, seem to doubt if they are permitted to distinguish the sentiments of such writers from the faith and practice of the Catholic Church. They have here the word of one who speaks with authority to correct so fundamental a mistake :—

> And now before I conclude these remarks, I must make one more observation relative to a practice which I consider to be one of the results of an unhealthy form of devotion. I allude to the practice which some people have of peremptorily setting down as un-Catholic, and anti-Roman, and contrary to the spirit of the Church, every practice and every teaching which does not coincide with their own views. Father Newman expresses himself unwilling to accept as oracles every opinion which is advocated by F. Faber or the *Dublin Review*, and forthwith Mr. Martin denounces him as anti-Roman and as a Jansenist. *Such tyrannical dogmatism is not to be tolerated.* The writers in the *Dublin Review* are good and talented men, and they have devoted their talents to the service of the Church, but the views they advocate are worth just as much as the arguments with which they support them, and no more. *If the subjects they treat are open subjects, they remain open subjects after they have been treated, just as much as they were before.* In like manner if any persons

find their devotion increased by the perusal of the books of F. Faber (and there are many who do), by all means let them use them; but let them not rashly judge others, who, finding no food for their devotion in such books, seek for it in others of a different stamp. It is not unfrequently said or hinted, that if a Protestant makes his submission to the Church, he is only half converted, and has not the true spirit of the Church, unless he is prepared to adopt for himself whatever practices of devotion he may find in use in Rome or in Catholic countries. Such teaching is not only prejudicial to enquirers, it is positively unsound. If a man has to be received into the Church, let him be instructed in the principles of true and solid devotion. Let him be taught to know and appreciate the hidden mysteries of the Adorable Sacrament and of the Sacred Heart of our Blessed Lord, also the high dignity and prerogatives of the Mother of God. Let him at the same time be instructed in the use of external means of devotion—the beads, sacred images, candles, flowers, canticles, etc. Let him clearly understand that these things are not to be valued for their own sake, but as means to an end, and it will not be long before such a one will be in the practice of a fervent, solid, Catholic devotion. If, on the other hand, a man will pin his devotion on some particular forms and practices, however good in themselves, simply because they are in use at Rome or elsewhere; *if he will persist in regarding as only half Catholics, and in calling hard names all those whose devotion runs in a groove different from his own*; of such a one it must be said, either that he has no real devotion, or at most that he has succeeded in reaching the very lowest phase of an unhealthy devotion. *

---

* *Tablet* for March 17. The italics are my own. A leading article in the same number, on Dr. Newman's assailant, contains the following broad and candid statement of the rights of free discussion, made with special reference to 'that school, or tendency, or party,' which the writer says has 'more repulsion than attraction for himself'; 'The preservation of its existence, its rights, its freedom, and the maintenance of fair play in its behalf, is a vital interest of ours and of everybody's.' No doubt, either school, or tendency, or party has the right to assert itself,

And, in illustration of the important distinction insisted on by the Bishop, as also by Dr. Newman, between English and foreign habits of thought, tastes, and virtues, and the folly of supposing that Catholic orthodoxy or devotion is inconsistent with hearty patriotism and sympathy with the national character of one's own country, I may quote the testimony of one of the most eminent German prelates of our day, whose words may have more weight with some, from his being considered the leading mind of what is there called Ultramontanism: 'We believe that Catholics should scrupulously avoid everything which can lead to the notion that they are strangers to the interests of Germany. We should carefully distinguish truth from error, *and not let any one surpass us in love for our country, its unity and its greatness.*' *

and to use its powers, whether of logic, or of rhetoric, or of criticism. If any author puts forth a book on one side, any author has a perfect right to do as much upon the other side. He may confute his adversary's statements, or may indirectly counteract their effect by an able and convincing exposition of his own views, in which those truths and principles which one side is apt to keep in the shade, are brought out into the fullest light in their most attractive form. And as one of the most efficient persuasives which men can use is the specification of the dangers and abuses to which an adversary's side is liable, no advocate is bound to renounce the use of this weapon.' He should, however, use it with discretion, and especially should refrain from imputing to his opponents meanings they themselves disclaim, or insisting on possible 'abuses' of their principles which do not appear to himself matter of practical danger.

* *Liberté, Autorité, Église.* Par. G. de Ketteler, Évêque de

It is no part of my present purpose to examine in detail all the difficulties that would have to be encountered in arranging our existing differences. They will occur readily enough to any one, and the more prominent of them have been lately set forth, from the Anglican point of view, with his accustomed vigour and moderation of statement, by a distinguished writer in the second series of Reunion Sermons, whom you have largely quoted; on the Catholic side by the Jesuit reviewer in the 'Études.'* Cardinal Wiseman, after referring to the inevitable opposition of the 'World' and 'the Enemy of good' to 'this holy work,' had spoken of 'sincere scruples about particular practices, unwillingness to surrender certain forms, the complicated questions of hierarchical arrangements, orders, and clerical discipline, and many others, *which it is needless to anticipate*, because they will soon enough show themselves.' † It would be both premature and unprofitable to discuss such points here, where I am concerned with principles rather than with the modes of applying them. But it is very observable that all these writers, as well as Dr. Pusey himself, keenly alive though they are to

---

Mayence. P. 223. Paris, 1862. I quote from the French authorised translation, not having access to the original. Further extracts will be found in the Appendix.

* *Sermons on Reunion*, Second Series, Sermon VII. by 'L.' Cf. *Etudes Relig.*, No. 38, pp. 261, sqq. Cf. also, for political aspects of the question, *Future Unity of Christendom*, by A. L. Phillips (de Lisle), pp. 48—50.

† *Letter to Lord Shrewsbury*, p. 39.

the gravity of the complications, steadily refuse to regard them as any valid objection to anticipating a prosperous result, and striving and praying for its accomplishment. Neither do I myself believe that, when once a sincere and practical *desire* for reconciliation makes itself felt on both sides, these difficulties of detail—chiefly concerning matters of variable *discipline*, which are, therefore, capable of readjustment—will be long in finding their solution. The old proverb is true in questions of public as well as of private interest, 'Where there's a *will* there's a *way*.' But there are two salient points of an abstract and dogmatic kind, one on our side, one on the Anglican, which seem at first sight to present such formidable impediments, that a few words may fairly be bestowed upon them here. I refer to the Thirty-nine Articles and the dogma of the Immaculate Conception. Most Catholics shrink with as much abhorrence from the former as most Anglicans have hitherto professed to do from the latter.

1. The Thirty-nine Articles are not a serious *crux*. There is high authority on both sides (as we have seen), including such names as Wiseman, Doyle, and Pusey, for considering that they may be so explained 'as to strip them of all opposition to the decrees of the Tridentine Synod.' Canon Estcourt, on the other hand, thinks that 'renouncing' them is an indispensable preliminary for reunion; and the 'Christian Remembrancer' agrees with him. Without presuming here to adjudicate between rival

authorities, it is obvious to remark that, whether or not the Articles are an insuperable bar to re-union, it is hardly conceivable that they should be long retained in a reunited Church; and for this simple reason, that nobody would care to retain them. Having premised thus much, I quote with sincere pleasure the following outspoken and generous statement of the 'Christian Remembrancer,' which is too important to be curtailed :—

When it is considered that the Articles were drawn up at a time when theology had reached nearly its lowest level in the Church of England, and were remodelled after the accession of Elizabeth, when the tone of religious belief was still lower, one is really tempted to ask with wonder, How is it that men have placed such implicit belief in them? And no answer can be given than that *they have been neglected and ignored.* Of course, there has been a large party who swear by them, and the existence of whose form of belief in the Church of England is guaranteed by their being retained; but it is impossible to deny that *they contain statements or implications that are verbally false, and others that are very difficult to reconcile with truth.* In the times that are coming over the Church of England the question will arise, *What service have the Articles of the Church of England ever done? And of what use are they at the present day?* The latter question must be answered very fully and satisfactorily, if the answer is to be any makeweight against the condemnation of them virtually pronounced by the 'Eirenicon.' We say *virtually*, for it is, after all, only an implicit, and not an explicit condemnation of them, that the volume contains. The slight difference of opinion (if difference there is as regards what the framers of the Articles intended) between ourselves and the respected author of the 'Eirenicon' need not be remarked on here. But we venture to go a step beyond any suggestion contained in this volume, and boldly proclaim our opinion, that before union with Rome can be effected, *the Thirty-nine Articles must be wholly withdrawn. They are virtually withdrawn at the present moment;*

for the very fact of the endorsement of the view of the 'Eirenicon' by its reviewer in the 'Times,' proves that, as far as the most important of them are concerned, there are persons who sign them in senses absolutely contradictory.

Such language, coming from such a quarter, is a sufficient guarantee that the Articles would not long be suffered by High Churchmen to stand in the way of any practical scheme of reconciliation; and the other great party in the Church of England had already indicated its desire to be freed from them.*

2. This is not the place to defend the dogma of the Immaculate Conception. I have had occasion to dwell on it in a previous work, and it has since been vindicated by Dr. Newman in a way that supersedes the necessity of any further comment. We are only concerned with it here in so far as it

* My extract is from the *Christian Remembrancer* for January, p. 188. The same number contains a favourable notice of Mr. Lee's reprint of Sancta Clara on the 39 Articles, as 'very important' in its bearing on their merely 'temporary and occasional character' (p. 243). The reader will not need to be reminded of Dean Milman's speech before the Royal Commission (afterwards published in *Macmillan's Magazine*), and Dean Stanley's letter to the Bishop of London to the same effect, to which may now be added his interesting paper on the *Eirenicon* in the April number of the *Contemporary Review*. As early as 1857 the *Edinburgh* had said of the 39 Articles, in an article on Convocation: 'They do not profess to be a Christian Creed. They are but a collection of propositions which, as matter of ecclesiastical *and political* regulation it was agreed should be enforced on all members of the Church of England, *i.e.*, *upon all Englishmen at the date of the Articles*, . . . which, *as matter of arrangement*, no one is to controvert, *not canons of faith* to be believed in order to salvation;'—which is much the argument of Tract 90.

may be considered a bar to reunion. Dr. Pusey has devoted over fifty pages of the 'Eirenicon' to a careful and elaborate analysis of the 'Doubts among the Roman Catholic Bishops, as to making the doctrine of the Immaculate Conception of the Blessed Virgin an Article of faith.' But he is too candid not to premise that these doubts referred in every instance to the *definition*, and not to the doctrine. And it would appear that his own objections and those of his numerous followers in the Church of England are of the same kind. They question the fitness of the belief for being made *de fide*, or the competence of the authority which defined it; they do not say the belief itself is false. I gather this, first from an important letter of Dr. Pusey's in the 'Guardian' of Jan. 24, which corrects a mistake in his book, and contains, in fact, a theological defence of the doctrine; secondly, from the language of the 'Christian Remembrancer,' which shall be quoted directly. Now if this be so, it is a very hopeful sign, when we recollect how, eleven years ago, every Anglican pulpit (by no means excepting those occupied by High Churchmen) rang with denunciations of 'the new dogma,' not only as unauthoritative, but as untrue—denunciations based, in nine cases out of ten, on the strangest misconceptions of its meaning.*

---

* Thus, e. g., a distinguished High Churchman of my acquaintance, who certainly had no wish to be unfair, preached a course of sermons on 'My spirit hath rejoiced in God *my Saviour*,' taking the last words as a conclusive refutation of the doctrine!

Very different and very cheering is the language of the leading High Church organ now:—

> It appears to us that the question [of the Immaculate Conception] *is absolutely open,* both in the Greek and English communions, simply on this ground, that neither in their Confession,* nor in our Articles, does this particular case appear to have been contemplated. The pious opinion so prevalent in the Roman Communion *seems to us allowable in the English.* . . . It seems to us just one of those cases where individuals have no power of judging for themselves, where they *may be well content to acquiesce in the decision of the Church of which they are members,* if such decision has already been pronounced, but which *they would do well to consider an open question,* unless they are sure such has been the case.

This is obviously the common-sense view of the matter for Anglicans, and it was very much my own ten years ago (when I fully believed the 'opinion' to be true, though not binding); but I more than doubt whether a single Anglican divine would then have publicly avowed it, still less the leading High Church Quarterly. Its open avowal now gives us good ground for hoping that, when our differences shall come to be considered κατὰ τὸ πρακτικὸν with a view to reconciliation, and when Anglicans become aware how completely the recent definition—apart from any question about the binding authority of Papal Bulls, as such—was endorsed, or rather anticipated, by the verdict of the *sensus fidelium,* they will not be unwilling to accept as a doctrine what

---

* The writer refers, I presume, to the 'Orthodox Confession,' sanctioned by the Synod of Bethlehem in 1672.

they are already learning to tolerate as a pious belief.

This leads me to say a word on a question already referred to, and which underlies all controversies about particular doctrines—I mean the principle of development, to which the Anglican Church is implicitly committed, just as much as we are, if only by her acceptance of the Nicene and Athanasian Creeds, but which it has been usual for her advocates very suicidally to disclaim. There are passages in the 'Eirenicon' which may be so interpreted, but they need not mean more than to repudiate what the author considers perversions of the principle. It is one thing to reject it, as laid down by such high authorities as Möhler, Döllinger, or Newman; quite another to protest against particular applications, or it may be caricatures, of it suggested by Dr. Pusey's evil genius of the 'Dublin.' And there is no direct reference, that I have discovered, to Dr. Newman's Essay from beginning to end of the volume. Meanwhile, there is direct evidence of a change coming over the mind of Anglicans on this matter. Out of eight reviews of an Essay of my own upon it last year, in various High Church organs, only *one* entered its protest against the abstract principle, and *five* distinctly admitted it, though they differed more or less, as was natural, from some parts of my treatment of it. And more than this, in an article on Lecky's 'History of Rationalism' in the current number of the 'Christian Remembrancer,' there occurs a passage on Development, so apposite in itself, and so accordant with what our own great theologians have maintained, that I shall venture to place it here side by side with a parallel passage from Döllinger's Speech on 'The Past and Present of Catholic Theology.' It is a complete endorsement of the *principle* of Dr. Newman's famous Essay by the same Review which twenty years ago so elaborately attacked it.

We are thus prepared to maintain that theology is science; and still further, that it is a *progressive* science. This may sound strange in ears accustomed to the *quod semper, quod ubique, quod ab omnibus*; but it is nevertheless true. What we mean, however, is deductive, not inductive, progress. There can be no progress in theology analogous to what takes place in chemistry. There can be no discovery of new facts from which we are to induce new laws; *but there is, and must be, a progress analogous to that, for instance, of geometry.* This progress consists in the gradual evolution of the fundamental ideas, the discovery of new relations involved in them, and new spheres in which they are valid. When Christianity was first introduced into the world, the whole mental condition of mankind was formed on a different model. The new ideas came in like a flash of light, and the soul opened to receive them. But it was not in the nature of things that they could at once be realized in all their fulness and in all their consequences. It was not possible that everything antagonistic to them could immediately vanish. *Ages were required to effect this.* There was a double progress, which went on simultaneously—the gradual evolution of the fundamental conceptions into clear light, the gradual throwing off of antagonistic traditions. Take the Church of the fourth century, as compared with the second. What an immense body of truth has already been attained *of which the previous time had no articulate conception*! How much clearer is the idea of God, and of the human soul! how much more free from opposing elements! How much more determined are the manifold relations, human and divine! In one point of view this additional truth is new; in another it is not new. It is new as a purely scientific progress; it is not new in regard to its elements. For all that the fourth century believed of God the second had received *implicitly* in the original revelation.*

Compare with this the following from Döllinger, and see if there be any substantial difference between them:—

> While we all in the Church recognise the principle of Tradition, and bear high upon our theological banner the inscription, *quod semper, quod ubique, quod ab omnibus*, this has often been misunderstood not only by opponents but by friends; as though Theology were to deal with the materials of Tradition like a miser who piles up a heap of coin in a jar and buries it in the earth. He certainly possesses a treasure, which neither increases nor diminishes, and can be dug up centuries afterwards, but which in the meantime remains dead and unproductive. But in the Church, and for her theology, tradition and its contents are *living and progressive*, combining rest and motion, stability and development, uniformity and variety. The traditional doctrine cannot act on mind and life, *without their reacting on it*. And its power of working on them rests chiefly on its containing in itself a germ of life in continuous internal activity.†

The writer goes on to observe—what may serve to reassure Dr. Pusey—that this process of development may be miserably perverted, 'under the manipulations of a crude, mechanical, *soi-disant*, conservative spirit;' and adds that ' examples are not far to seek *now*, as formerly, of theologians who turn their material into pebbles instead of jewels, and of whom one is constrained to say, Nihil tetigit quod non deornavit.' Absit omen!

* *Chr. Rem.* Jan. 1866, p. 231.
† *Die Vergangenheit urd Gegenwart der kathol. Theol.* p. 27.

While touching on the difficulties of Reunion, it may be well to notice one very plausible objection not unfrequently urged against the particular scheme for reuniting the great Episcopal bodies indicated in Dr. Pusey's book, and which has formed the immediate, though not exclusive, object of daily intercession for nine years past to an Association numbering now many thousands of members, and originally founded in this country, in simple reliance on the Divine promise, at a period when no word of encouragement had for several years fallen from any influential personage, either among Anglicans or among ourselves; when certainly the most sanguine could not anticipate the phenomenon we have witnessed, of the appearance and reception of Dr. Pusey's book, and of the Reunion literature it is creating, which shows it to be indeed a touchstone whereby the thoughts of many hearts are revealed. It has then been said both by Catholics and Anglicans, and said with perfect truth, that no reunion could be adequate or complete which failed to include, not only the three great bodies which have retained at least the form of Episcopal organization, but also the outlying Protestant communities, whether here or abroad, which have rejected the very idea of a priesthood and a Visible Church. I quite share this feeling; and I therefore not only hail, in one sense, with sincere satisfaction, such apparitions as the Irvingite movement or the Evangelical Alliance, but gladly recognised the genuine though eccentric manifestation of a desire for unity in the recent proposal of a Dissenting Minister to hold a 'Catholic Church Congress,' from which none but Catholics were to be excluded. And I shall give in an Appendix some striking passages from the works of Dr. Döllinger, referring primarily and directly to the restoration he so greatly desires of the German 'Evangelical Church' to Catholic unity; an object which, as you will remember, the great Bossuet in his own day laboured to accomplish. Dr. Pusey refers to the same thing, quoting Cardinal Wiseman and Möhler.*

But we do not need Aristotle's weighty authority to remind us that, while the end comes first in the order of our thoughts, the means for attaining it come first in our practical endeavours; and our own English proverb will tell us that 'half a loaf is better than no bread.' Now a reunion of Catholics, Easterns, and Anglicans would be a great deal more than half a loaf. Of the third of the human race, numbering roughly about three hundred millions, who profess Christianity of some kind, at least two hundred and fifty millions, or five-sixths, are included in those three bodies.† To reunite them would be at once to join the immense majority of Christians in one visible fold. More than that, it would give to the Church such a moral preponderance as could hardly fail to tell at no distant period on those without her pale.

* *Eirenicon*, p. 259. Cf. *Letter to Lord Shrewsbury*, p. 33.

† It seems that a full third of British subjects, including Ireland and the Colonies, are Catholics. See *Future Unity of Christendom*, p. 59.

'Dissent would break in pieces *beneath the silent action of universal attraction.*'* Nor is this all. If the Apostle bids do good first to those who are of the household of faith, we are surely acting in the spirit of his injunction when we seek first to bring in those who are nearest to our doors. The Greek Church certainly possesses, and the Anglican as certainly claims, a common point of fellowship with us in the possession of a true priesthood. And, whatever judgment may be formed as to the precise nature and degree of moral guilt involved in the Oriental or Anglican Schism, or on the vexed question of Anglican orders, and the like, no rational man will doubt —nor does any one that I know of pretend to question—that both Greeks and Anglicans have far more in common with the Catholic Church than any of the separated Protestant communities, British or Continental. Our Archbishop, who will hardly be accused of excessive Anglican partialities, admits this expressly as regards the Church of England in his recent Pastoral, though he observes, very naturally, that the millions who are in separation from it have also claims upon us.† There is often much soreness felt among Anglicans at what they call the repudiation of their Baptism and Orders. As regards the latter point, *adhuc sub judice lis est.* By all means let the evidence be brought into court; it will be our duty

---

* *Letter to Lord Shrewsbury*, p. 41. Cf. *Future Unity of Christendom*, p. 50 : 'Although the dissenters would still remain in theory as they are, yet *the moral force of dissent would be gone.*'
† *Reunion of Christendom*, p. 14.

to examine it, which has not yet been done, and to judge accordingly.* The validity of Baptism administered with the right matter and form is absolutely certain, quite irrespectively of the priestly (or Christian) character of the person who confers it. The rule for *conditional* rebaptism of converts was first introduced, I believe, in this country some sixty years ago, from a suspicion (whether reasonable or not is immaterial here) that the sacrament was often so carelessly administered as to make it practically doubtful in any given case whether the essential conditions had been complied with. And this is a question not of doctrine but of fact. Rebaptism of converts is always conditional, and is omitted where evidence is forthcoming of the validity of the previous administration. There are some very temperate remarks on the question of Anglican Sacraments in the second of the articles so often quoted in the 'Études Religieuses.'

I may suitably refer here to the words of a distinguished leader of the extreme Ultramontane party—so far as a man of his commanding genius can be identified with any particular party—who was the pioneer of what is usually called the 'Catholic reaction' following on the religious cataclysm of the French Revolution. The words have, I am aware, often been quoted before, but they are too weighty to suffer from repetition, nor is their force likely to be

* I am glad to see that a work on the subject by the Rev. F. G. Lee is in course of preparation. Has the Eastern Church taken any definite line either way about it?

weakened by the shallow sneer of a prejudiced critic, which I read the other day with considerable amusement, that as De Maistre had never himself been an Anglican, his judgment on the matter was worthless! His words are these, and they sound almost like a prophecy :—

> If ever Christians should approach each other—and every consideration might urge them to do so—it would seem that the first advance should be made by the Church of England. . . . The Anglican Church *which touches us with one hand, touches with the other those we cannot touch*; and although from one point of view she is exposed to the attacks of both sides, and presents the somewhat ludicrous spectacle of a rebel preaching obedience, yet under other aspects *she is very precious*, and may be considered as one of those chemical intermediary substances capable of combining elements which have a natural repulsion to each other.*

I am but subscribing to the sentiments of this keen observer of social, political, and religious phenomena, when I avow my deliberate conviction, which is the growth of years, that the only available method, humanly speaking, for restoring England, with her multitudinous sects, to the great commonwealth of Christendom, is through the medium of her National Church. If the avowal is regarded by any one (by you I am sure it will not be) as a mark of prejudice, or insularity, or 'incompetence,' or 'unsoundness,' or 'spiritual rebellion,' I am sorry for it; but 'facts are stubborn things,' and it will not be the first time I have been called hard names for saying what men of high standing and unim-

---

* *Considérations sur la France*, c. 2.

peachable orthodoxy have said before me, and what I firmly believe to be the truth. Dr. Pusey's view of the way in which the Church of England may be expected to subserve the restoration of Christian unity seems to coincide very much with De Maistre's. He says, in a letter to the 'Guardian' of Jan. 24: 'What I trust God the Holy Ghost is calling us to, is to seek a healthful reunion and intercommunion with other Catholics in East and West [i.e., with the Catholic and Greek Church], whatever office we may, in God's good purpose, have *towards the Protestants* [i.e., the non-episcopal bodies], *will be after, not before*, our reunion with the rest of Catholic Christendom.' I take up again the words of our friend Mr. de Lisle, more applicable now than when they were originally spoken in 1841; 'The English Church never can be Catholic while she remains in her present position—*isolated, separated from the rest of Christendom*. . . . Let her remember that the eyes of Catholic Christendom are fixed upon her, watching whether yet again she will join their vast communion. *It is in her power to do so.* . . . Let her not disappoint the universal hope of Christendom.'*

Dr. Pusey will indeed reply that the divisions of Christendom are the common penalty of a common sin, and that the Church of England committed no act of schism. He not only denies that in the Eastern

---

* *Remarks on Letter to Jelf*, p. 22.

Schism 'the whole guilt of this miserable rent has fallen upon one side only,' which few would maintain, but insists that the abuses admitted on all hands to exist justified the Church of England in separately reforming herself, and that she did not any more reject 'a visible head,' or sever herself from the Roman See, than the African Church did in St. Augustine's time. To me, as to yourself, this last statement does 'sound strangely paradoxical.' But I accept its *animus* as an augury for the future, while unable to appreciate its accuracy in the past. It would be quite foreign to my present purpose to enter on the theological or controversial bearings of the question as regards the Roman Primacy,* or the English schism. But on the historical domain we may find, in Möhler's language, 'a common point of meeting, where the open confession of mutual guilt will be followed by the festival of reconciliation.' † It has been fully and freely admitted, at least since the passions and polemics of the Reformation period passed away, by all the most eminent Catholic writers, that the breach was precipitated, if not occasioned, by the gravest faults on *both* sides, and that, while on the part of the seceders it was a revolt against the divine authority of the Church, it

---

* I say 'primacy,' for the word 'supremacy,' of which Dr. Pusey speaks, is unknown to theology and to the Canons. See *Études Rel.*, No. 39, p. 379.

† *Symbolism*, vol. ii. p. 32 (English translation). Cf. *Letter to Lord Shrewsbury*, p. 33.

was also God's righteous judgment on the sins of her rulers and her children. Confessions of this sort were common enough at the time among the most distinguished churchmen;* in our own day they have been emphatically repeated by such men as Möhler, Cardinal Wiseman, and Döllinger, as will be seen from the Appendix, and might be more fully illustrated from their writings. On the other hand, we have the following remarkable admission from the great heresiarch himself in the earlier stages of his career, in 1519, when he thought the Pope was either 'Antichrist himself, or his apostle,' and yet wrote: 'That the Roman Church is more honoured by God than any other *is not to be doubted.* St. Peter, St. Paul, forty-six popes, some hundreds of thousands of martyrs, have laid down their lives in its communion, having overcome hell and the world; so that the eyes of God rest on the Roman Church with special favour. *The worse things are going, the more we should hold close to it*; for it is not by separation from it *that we can make it better*.'† *O si sic omnia!* And if the Reformation was a judgment, we need not shrink from admitting, what immediately follows, that it has also entailed a serious loss not only of numerical but of moral strength. When Dr. Pusey observes (p. 188) that

---

* Some striking examples are given in Ffoulke's *Christendom's Divisions.*

† D'Aubigné's *Life of Luther*, vol. ii. p. 16, quoted in Gladstone's *Church Principles*, p. 293.

'the Saxon mind is a large element in the Christian body,' he is but endorsing the words of the great Catholic apologist: 'I trust that all European races will ever have a place in the Church; and assuredly I think that *the loss of the English, not to say the German element, in its composition, has been a most serious evil.*'* Each great family of nations, as the Aryan or Semitic, has its special gift from God, and therefore its special office and work in the Universal Church. And so, again, to the Oriental mind, with its subtle spirit of abstract speculation, it was given to investigate the mysteries of the Divine nature, and to elaborate the early creeds; to the Latin mind, which did not lose under the Gospel the stern objectivity that had been its characteristic all along, we owe what is sometimes called the anthropological side of our theology, treating of the powers and corruption of the human will, and the operations of sacramental grace; the Teutonic mind, with its stubborn energy, and honest love of truth, has chiefly busied itself with the subjective aspects of religion, the sacredness of individual responsibility, and the inalienable sovereignty of conscience. But this last process has been carried on, for the most part, outside the Church, and too often in hostility to her. Nor can it be other than a serious misfortune that those critical and exegetical studies which have made such immense strides in our own day should have been mostly divorced from the doctrinal sanctions

* *Apologia*, p. 412.

and uninfluenced by the religious atmosphere of Catholicism, and thus have involved the whole subject in suspicion of error, instead of being invaluable auxiliaries to the cause of truth. It would surely be no light gain were the Teutonic spirit of freedom and searching inquiry no longer the foe or the rival, but the trusted handmaid of the Church. We need not, then, scruple to admit what Dr. Pusey reminds us, that 'pious Roman Catholics have felt before' (as how, indeed, should they not?) that 'mutual weakness, and injury to faith, and morals, and life,' are the fruit of division; while 'the strength is wasted against each other which should be concentrated against the common foe of Jesus and of all who are His.' The *organic reunion* of Christendom is the only adequate remedy for these crying evils: 'a better management of our differences' is a most desirable preliminary to this, but can never be a substitute for it. And thus I am brought to say something directly of the benefits that might be expected to accrue from Reunion. For as early Church history is a conspicuous illustration of the first half of the saying of the Roman historian, '*Concordiâ res parvæ crescunt*,' so the last three centuries supply a terrible comment on the second, '*Discordiâ etiam magnæ dilabuntur.*' To enumerate the curses entailed by division is to indicate the blessings which union alone can bring.

1. In a treatise like the present I cannot, of course, pretend to do more than roughly sketch outlines

which every thoughtful man will easily fill in for himself; and I shall continue to abstain from strictly theological considerations, as foreign to my purpose. To come first, then, to what lies on the surface and is suggested by my last extract from the 'Eirenicon,' who can forecast the incalculable accession of moral strength that would result, negatively, from the mere fact of that *waste* of energy on all sides—which is an inevitable result of our divisions—being checked? It was an observation of Sir Isaac Newton's, that any one might have made the discoveries he did who would only *attend*, i. e. concentrate his mind on one point. And the gain would undoubtedly be immense, beyond what we can even imagine, if the religious energies of Christendom were concentrated on a common purpose and a common truth, instead of being frittered away on the pitiful but pressing exigencies of internal struggle and defence. Concentration is the nearest approach in created beings to that divine 'simplicity' which theology teaches us to revere as among the grandest attributes of God. What broke the power of ancient Greece? What made Italy 'a geographical expression'? Why is Germany, as such, a political cipher on the map of modern Europe? What was the secret of Rome's imperial power which Satan has borrowed for the confusion of Christendom? *Divide et impera.* What was the predestined curse of Ishmael and his race? That his hand should be against every man, and every man's hand against him. Why was the force of the Reformation spent, as Macaulay has so pointedly reminded us, before it was half a century old? Because those who agreed that Rome was Antichrist could agree in nothing else. Why are the records of so many Protestant missionaries a confession or a catalogue of failures? Because 'they fell out by the way.' And why—for the suffering is not all on one side—is every Catholic country in Europe honeycombed with open or secret infidelity? Because twice the energy has been exhausted in contending with Protestants that might have won the irreligious and cut up the roots of unbelief. It is, in the words of the eloquent spokesman of the French episcopate, 'this anarchy which is the source of our weakness, and the most active solvent of all religious faith.'*

2. Closely connected with this negative evil of disunion is a positive evil, in the temper and line of action it creates and fosters. Jesus prayed His disciples might be one, that the world might recognise His divine mission; the badge of their discipleship was to be that they loved one another. But the world has long since learnt to reverse the old proverb; and men exclaim in sorrow, or in mockery, or in triumph, as the case may be, 'See how these Christians *hate* one another.' A Free Kirk minister lately prayed : ' *O that we were all baptized into the spirit of disruption* '! To the same effect is a story current in London, not many years ago, of a Jewish lady re-

* *La Convention et l'Encyclique*, par l'Évêque d'Orléans, p. 126.

marking to a Protestant acquaintance, who expressed a repugnance to being in the same room with a Catholic dignitary: 'You will not of course expect me to enter into your *Christian* feelings.' Three centuries of bitter hate have but too well justified the sarcasm. Is it not almost time we should think of trying to disprove it? For this, be it remembered, is no mere matter of feeling, or abstract opinion; it controls our whole religious ἦθος, shapes our policy, colours our literature, regulates our charities, limits our sense of justice, rearranges our standard of veracity, almost articulates our prayers. We have a graduated scale of morality for our theological dealings with friend or foe, and receive the Decalogue with an unwritten gloss. We are adepts in the forbidden science of Job's advisers, and think it a pious obligation to 'speak deceitfully for God.' We are slow to allow that anything on our side can be wrong, and loud in asserting that nothing on the other side can be right. It is Dr. Arnold, I think, who somewhere says that he should have more confidence in the great Anglican divines if they occasionally admitted that their Church was not absolutely perfect; and Macaulay clenches his criticism by a characteristic sneer at the ostentatious disclaimer of infallible guidance by those who are never in the wrong. The sneer is not unmerited, but it has a wider application. The works of mediæval writers and acts of mediæval Councils literally bristle with denunciations of ecclesiastical abuses and energetic demands for their reformation.

There is abundant censure of corruptions and ridicule of failures in the works of modern controversialists of every school; but the corruptions are to be seen in rival communions, and the failures are exhibited to illustrate the triumphs of their own. We all have too much of the spirit of the Church of Laodicea, and think we 'are rich and have need of nothing.' We forget that golden saying of De Maistre's, 'The Church has need of truth, *and of that alone.*' And in all this there is a double sin which works a double punishment. We are afraid to confess, and therefore powerless to correct, what is amiss among ourselves; and we are cherishing that evil spirit of ἐπιχαιρεκακία, condemned by even Heathen moralists, which leads us rather to rejoice in exaggerating the faults than in discovering the merits of those who are separated from us. And such a temper tends to poison the very springs of moral and spiritual life. The distinguished layman who is so bright an ornament of the French Church, while yet he has never ceased to testify his 'ardent and profound sympathy for the great nation, Christian and free,' to which he is joined by ties both of friendship and of blood, may teach us a noble lesson here. I quote from his famous pamphlet on the Indian Debate, first published in the 'Correspondant.' 'For my part, I say it plainly, *I have a horror of that orthodoxy which takes no account of justice and truth, humanity and honour;* and I am never weary of repeating those bold words recently uttered by the Bishop of La Rochelle (in the 'Univers' of August 10, 1858) : "Would it not be well to give some Catholics a course of lectures on the virtues of the natural order—respect for our neighbour, loyalty in dealing with our opponents, the spirit of equity and charity? ... The virtues of the natural order are essential, and the Church herself can give no dispensation from their observance."* Three-fourths of the incentives to the shocking temper Montalembert denounces, would cease to exist in a reunited Christendom.

3. It can only be because the experience of centuries has accustomed us to so strange a phenomenon, that we have come to consider the nominal Christianity of a bare third of the human race an adequate fulfilment of the Divine commission to 'make disciples of all nations,' and the Divine assurance that 'the kingdoms of the world are become the kingdoms of our Lord and of His Christ.' We turn with weariness or impatience from prophecies which can only be explained of our present state, by being explained away; and are content to leave them for the battlefield of rival fanatics, each more irrational than the last. No strange interpretation, however wild, need surprise us, while the true solution is yet to come; not even though we witness the tercentenary of a tradition—which has before now ensnared the highest intellects and saddened the noblest hearts—bidding us recognise the pre-

* *Correspondant*, Oct. 1858, pp. 211, 212.

dicted Antichrist and the 'Man of Sin' in the Primatial See of Christendom, the Rock whereon the Church was built. Glorious, indeed, beyond all human praise have been the efforts of Catholic missionaries in the present and the past, and few are the Heathen shores that have not been consecrated by the passion-blood of their generous martyrdom. The Church which counts Xavier and Francis of Assisi among her Saints can be charged with no niggard zeal for the conversion of the idolater or the Turk. And none who have knelt (as I have) in the *Salle des Martyres* at Paris, will say that zeal is quenched. The name of Henry Martyn would alone vindicate Protestants from the reproach of ignoring so solemn a Christian obligation; and the enormous sums annually subscribed in England for missionary objects are an honour to our country. But Catholic missions have had only a partial and precarious success, while the failure of Protestant missions has almost passed into a proverb. Why is this? The answer stares us in the face throughout the length and breadth of Heathendom. Jesus prayed His followers might be one, 'that the world may believe that Thou hast sent Me.' He prayed for their visible unity *as a public witness to mankind.* And so long as that unity lasted, the world listened to their message. The huge fabric of the old Roman Empire succumbed to the preaching of Apostles and Evangelists, who taught in many tongues a common faith, and sealed their testimony with their blood.

Our Saxon forefathers, in England and in Germany, were converted by the Apostles of the mediæval Church; for the unity of the West was still unbroken, and Augustine and Boniface were confronted by no rival preachers of 'another Gospel, which yet is not another.' But when Christian missioners are heard to denounce one another, and altar is set up against altar, and the very Heathen have learnt (it would seem) to give distinctive nicknames to the churches of conflicting creeds, can we marvel if they turn with indifference or contempt from a religion which to their eyes is divided against itself? Can we be surprised if they mistrust a message which is variously delivered by discordant lips, and refuse to acknowledge His Divine mission, whose professed ambassadors dispute about their own? I trow not. They may well reply to us with the Patriarch of old, 'Sirs, ye are brethren,' and bid us first be agreed among ourselves before we ask them to adopt our faith. Let no one object that I am denying the unity of the Church, which is an article of the Creed. But the unity of the Church, from which *a full third* of baptized Christians are divided—I care not to wrangle over the precise figures—*has ceased to be a witness to Heathendom.* I take up again the words of the great French Prelate already referred to: 'What would not be our power for preaching the Gospel to those who know it not, *if we were at one among ourselves!* The majority of mankind remain buried in darkness, because we bring them a

Gospel divided, disputed, cut up into fragments Oh, *if England, France, and Russia were agreed in the truth*, and, therefore, in the charity and zeal of the apostolate, the face of the East—of the whole world—would be changed!'* If experience goes for anything, if prophecy goes for anything, if the words of Jesus have any meaning, the world will not be converted till Christendom is at unity with itself.

4. But it is not only Heathendom that needs conversion, or Buddhists and savages alone whose unbelief is perpetuated by our internal divisions. There is another consideration too which cannot but have its weight with all who know anything of the force of human sympathy, or of that higher law of charity revealed by Christ. We need not look beyond our own beloved country, or even this Christian metropolis, for an illustration of what I mean. It is not many months since civilized English society was shuddering at the hideous spectacle—indicated rather than displayed in the graphic sketch of an adventurous philanthropist—of that seething mass of social and moral depravity which flows beside our footsteps, and is centred round our homes; and it may well be hoped that the impression then produced will not be exhausted in gazing at the photographs of 'Daddy' and the blue-eyed hero of the 'rummy songs' which decorate our shop windows,

* *La Convention et l'Encyclique*, p. 127.

or even in the noble efforts since commenced to rescue the 'Homeless Boys' from the streets of London.* Yet the story—so terribly suggestive in its unadorned simplicity—told us little we might not have known or confidently surmised before. Poor young Kay and his fellow-denizens of the Casual Ward are after all but average specimens, scarcely perhaps unfavourable ones, of the thousands and tens of thousands whom we, intent on our bitter controversies, have suffered to grow up worse than Heathen in the midst of this Christian land. For how can such phenomena be dealt with by rival sects at internecine strife with each other? How at all except by taking, in nautical language, 'a long pull, and a strong pull, *and a pull all together*'? Half the energy that is wasted year by year on mutual recrimination and defence might convert a million of these spiritual pariahs to the love and worship of that Sacred Name they never knew, or know only to blaspheme. The moral Heathenism, with all its nameless horrors, which is the standing scandal of Christian cities, of Christian lands, results from the disunion of Christians. Surely we may well say, with the Prince of the Apostles, 'It is time for judgment *to begin from the House of God.*' † I trust indeed, nay I firmly believe (it would be agony to doubt it), that countless multitudes of those whom

---

* Our Archbishop has also come forward to plead the spiritual claims of these neglected children.

† 1 Pet. iv. 17.

we have left to blaspheme His Name on earth, who in spiritual discernment 'know not their right hand from their left,' will be cleansed by the compassionate touch of what Faber somewhere beautifully calls 'that eighth sacrament of fire,' and will kneel hereafter among His ransomed children before the throne of God and of the Lamb. But what judgment shall be passed on those who needlessly prolong, or will not help to reconcile, the divisions which leave them to die in their sins? He who chose publicans for His Apostles, a converted prostitute to stand beneath His Cross, Pagan soldiers for His dying intercession, and a forgiven murderer to be the first with Him in Paradise, had no gentler greeting for the Pharisees, who 'sat in Moses' seat,' than 'hypocrites,' 'serpents,' 'blind guides,' 'brood of vipers,' 'children of hell.' Let us look to it; for we are bickering on the brink of a volcano, and we pay for the cherished luxury of cursing one another with 'slaves and souls of men.'

5. So much for that moral Heathenism which is the plague-spot of our Christian cities. Last, but not least, there is the growing scepticism of our educated and half-educated classes. That is the direct, the inevitable product of our divided state. Intellectual difficulties must always find a natural ally in the infirmity of a perverted will. The argument for God and holiness has at best to fight against fearful odds; but its strength is doubly paralysed when the united forces of moral and

mental uncertainty are pitted against evidence discredited by the disputes of the witnesses. It is so obvious a resource to stand aloof from rival claimants on your allegiance; so plausible to balance with impartial scorn the merits and demerits of conflicting creeds. The 'Secularist' lecturers, who are hired to preach atheism every Sunday in all our principal cities, know that well enough, and are not slow to avail themselves of their knowledge. There is, indeed, a path of simplicity and obedience, wherein 'the wayfarers, though fools, shall not err;' there is guidance now, as in the Psalmist's day, for 'the meek and gentle.' Yet too often and too naturally, the young, the brave, the generous, are misled through what is noblest in their nature amid the strife of tongues, and fall back at last on 'honest doubt' as the substitute for faith, instead of being one of the roads to it. And how much more the baser minds, who must ever be the numerical majority, whose pride is offended by the 'foolishness' of the Gospel message, or their darling lusts crossed by its uncompromising strictness, and who gladly recognise in the multiplicity of discordant teachings a decent excuse—perhaps even to their own consciences,—though not a justification, for ignoring all alike. This, alas! is no fancy picture. Scepticism advances with swift though noiseless tide among our literary men, our men of business, our lawyers, our clerks in public offices, our medical students, our artizans, among even the youth of our

Universities; it advances, perhaps, most swiftly among the young, who in other days were the foremost champions, the boldest martyrs of the faith. And if this is true of England, those who know best assure us that it is truer still elsewhere. Who then will refuse to respond to the touching appeal which closes the 'Eirenicon': 'The strife with unbelief stretches and strains the powers of the Church *everywhere*; Satan's armies are united, at least in their warfare against ' the truth as it is in Jesus.' *Are those who would maintain the faith in Him alone to be at variance?* '* Quod semper, quod ubique, quod ab omnibus forms a threefold cord that is not easily broken. But for centuries now antiquity, authority, and reason have *seemed*, to the outward eye, to be unnaturally divorced from one another. Authority is the attribute of Catholicism; ancient precedent, to its minutest details, is the boasted heirloom of the Greeks; reason is the plea of Protestantism. Not, of course, that Catholicism is really unreasonable or novel, or that the Greeks do not lay claim to authority, or Protestants appeal to history: but that these elements of influence, which ought to work harmoniously together, have come to be regarded as the special boast, and appear to many the separate possession, of rival claimants on their faith. Proofs, however cogent, of the dogmatic authority of the Church are found no adequate counterpoise to the exigence of visible

* *Eirenicon*, p. 335.

facts. And thus, all who feel any inclination to doubt, and many who desire to believe, are perplexed and alienated. Disunion is the opportunity of unbelief.

To these prominent evils of disunion, which lie on the surface and must strike the most casual observer, might be added many more, less conspicuous but not less real. Thus, I suppose, the average standard of Christian holiness is almost inevitably lowered, even for those who are not themselves severed from the Apostolic fellowship or the grace of the Sacraments, in a state of society like the present, where religious *esprit de corps* in its least amiable form is so largely obtruded on our thoughts, and almost intermingled with our prayers. It is the remark of a writer who has of late attracted considerable attention, that very few of the greatest heroes of Paganism can properly be called *holy*, whereas holiness is the characteristic product of the Gospel of Christ, and has been in all ages widely exemplified among His disciples.* The corrupt civilisation of ancient Rome could not resist this crucial test of the moral superiority of its antagonist. Christianity owed its triumph over the convictions and consciences of men less to the skill of its apologists or the zeal of its preachers, than to

---

* *Ecce Homo*, p. 171. The assertion that there were ' *scarcely one or two* ' among ' all the men of the ancient heathen world ' who could be called 'holy,' is surely too sweeping. More names than that will occur at once to almost every student of antiquity.

the blood of its Martyrs and the patience of its Saints. The words of its Divine Founder were a prediction as well as a counsel: 'By their fruits ye shall know them.' Can the same argument be pleaded with like effect against the modern rivals of the Church's claims? Saints, no doubt, there are, now as ever, uncertified often by outward sign, in the cloister, in the desert, at the altar, in the privacy of Christian homes, amid the busy throng of men. But the world does not instinctively take knowledge of us, as it did of the first believers, that we 'have been with Jesus.' The first great schism which rent the unity of Christendom found its formal pretext in a dispute about the Procession of the Holy Spirit who is the Bond of Unity in the Godhead and Source of sanctity to man.* The records of every Council, general or provincial, from Vienne to Trent, will tell us, in language that cannot be mistaken, what shocking corruptions preceded, though they did not justify, the second. And what was urged as the excuse has been the abiding consequence of schism. In the words of Luther, already quoted, which he unfortunately lived to forget, 'The worse things are going, the more we should hold close to the Church; *for it is not by*

---

* It is surely a mistake of Dean Stanley to say (*Contemporary Review*, p. 548) that the *Filioque* was ' *introduced* with the *express object* of condemning [the Eastern] Churches.' It was first introduced in Spain at the third Council of Toledo, 589 A.D., and not sanctioned till long afterwards by the Holy See; and at Florence the Greeks were not required to insert the words in their Creed.

separation from it that we can make it better,'—or, he might have added, ourselves.

It is too obvious to require being dwelt upon, that theological inquiries would be prosecuted with far more powerful machinery, and more real and permanent success, if Christendom were again one great commonwealth of letters, with division of labour but perfect harmony of aim. The gigantic resources expended by rival theologians on purely controversial argument—doomed for the most part to perish with the using—would be jointly employed on elaborating from common principles the science which developes and illustrates the doctrines of a common faith. And that huge critical apparatus, which has been the chief contribution and most effective weapon of Protestant theology, would be used henceforth in no spirit of jealous antagonism or barren negation, but in the service of the Church, and for the promotion and recommendation of Christian truth. We should hear less of the unnatural conflict between Science and Revelation; and the master intellects of the age would feel it no degradation to bow, like Augustine or Aquinas, before the divine mysteries of Faith.

Neither, again, would the concentration and better organised appliance of all our available energies for the moral, social, and spiritual improvement of the ignorant and suffering be a slight advantage. On this point Cardinal Wiseman has insisted so strongly in his Letter to Lord Shrewsbury, that a passing reference will be sufficient here. There is no people so quick in its sympathies or so generous in its charities as our own. Were those charities exercised within the sphere of Catholic unity, and made subservient to the highest interests of religious truth, England might regain her glorious name among the nations, and be called once more the Isle of Saints.

One objection, indeed, there is to the force, or at least the relevancy of all that has been said, which is often felt even when it is not put into words. I seem to hear around me a chorus of 'airy tongues' —scornful, angry, impatient, sorrowful—that syllable the hopeless names, 'visionary,' 'Quixotic,' 'enthusiast.' I seem to see fingers as of a man's hand writing over the portals of every church in Christendom the fatal legend,

Lasciate ogni speranza, voi ch' entrate !

From Babel downwards history is a record of 'confusion,' but the streams once parted have never joined again. The temple of God was in Jerusalem, but the worship of Gerizim outlived its fall; unity is the primal attribute of the Church, but division is the normal state, almost the boast, of Christendom, and the Council of Florence revealed without reversing it. The fruitless aspirations of Contarini, or Bossuet, or Leibnitz, are honourable to those who entertained them, and show that their zeal exceeded their common sense. Sooner shall the lion and the lamb lie down together, than Catholic, Greek, and Protestant lay aside their immemorial feuds. Why set your teeth on edge with sour grapes? Why sow a crop of vain enthusiasm, to reap a harvest of disappointment? Such is the objection urged—clamorously, courteously, contemptuously, as the case may be—on every side. Few words will suffice to answer it. History *is* a record of divisions; 'jealousy *is* cruel as the grave;' schemes of reunion *have* often failed. I admit it all—what then? Is prophecy become an old almanac? Have the words of Jesus lost their meaning? Are there mountains prayer can *not* remove? Is there something after all that *is* impossible with God? What Christian dares to say so?

But you tell us we are enthusiasts. I accept the name, I glory in it. If that be a reproach, we are content to share it with the best, the greatest, the noblest of every age. Nothing great was ever done in the world or in the Church without enthusiasm, and nothing ever will be. If the Apostles had felt no enthusiasm,

> No angry world had risen to hate and slay,
> *And thou hadst been a Heathen in thy day.*

The power which created Christendom can alone reunite it. St. Philip Neri used to say that with twelve men whose enthusiasm was all for God he would undertake to convert the world. Enthusiasm —I say it with reverence—is the very life of the Church. The Church that had no enthusiasm was bidden to repent, or Christ would cast it out of His

mouth. 'He contemplated a Church in which the enthusiasm of humanity should not be felt by two or three only, but widely. *For a lukewarm Church He would not condescend to legislate.*' And, as the same writer reminds us, 'One power enthusiasm has almost without limit—the power of propagating itself—and it was for this that Christ depended on it.' *
Ours is an age of enthusiasms—literary, scientific, artistic, political—each admirable in its way; of philanthropic enthusiasms nobler still, but too often disjoined from love to Him who is the true Root of humanity.† Why cannot we have an enthusiasm for God and for our brethren, an enthusiasm for the honour of Jesus in the fulfilment of His dying prayer? 'Despair is still'—for despair is the temper of devils. Hope is the virtue of Christians, and hope without enthusiasm is dead. 'All things are possible to him that believeth,' but prayer without enthusiasm is not the prayer of faith. The first condition of all acceptable service to Christ is loyalty, and the deepest disloyalty is not to trust His promises.

But is there nothing in the outward aspect of

---

* *Ecce Homo*, p. 256.

† There is a truth in Mr. Lecky's statement, though (like many of his statements) it is an exaggeration, when he says, 'Liberty, not theology, is the enthusiasm of the nineteenth century. The very men who would once have been conspicuous saints are now conspicuous revolutionists.' There are points of contact between the characters of St. Bernard and Garibaldi. Shelley had the making of a saint in him.

things for hope to feed upon? Look back on that dreary century of 'light without love,' which came next before our own, when Christian faith seemed to be dying out by inches in the very heart of the Christian Church. Look at its stormy close when the 'eldest daughter of the Church' had renounced her creed, when Heathen deities were borne in solemn procession through the streets of a Christian capital, and the goddess Reason enthroned on the altar of its cathedral. Or, turn your eyes on England when Wesley was cast out of the National Church for preaching the love of Jesus, when the test of orthodoxy was to abjure enthusiasm, and belief in the Sacraments was chiefly valued as a safeguard against belief in converting grace. Think of the time within our own memory when the Apostolic Succession was the doctrinal limit of High Church aspirations, and preaching in the surplice of their ritual. And then consider the 'Eirenicon,' and how it has been received in the country and the Church of England—how Catholic teaching gains ground daily in her pulpits, and Catholic ceremonial at her altars. Ponder over the changes that have passed in the lifetime of the great Christian poet, who even now, as I am writing, has been taken from us, as we may well hope and believe, to keep his Easter in a brighter home, after living to see the religious affections of two successive generations of Englishmen tuned to the music of his song. Remember, too, how fast we live, if I may be allowed the expression, as compared with our fathers. Our decades are their centuries. Then, again, increased facilities of communication between different countries are rapidly breaking down barriers of national and local prejudice, and in religious matters as in secular, isolation is the strength of schism. Observe how the old hateful spirit of persecution is dying out everywhere; how even amid the most fundamental differences men are trying to understand one another better. The recent undertaking, commenced under the high sanction of the Archbishop of Paris, for a French translation of the Bible by a combined body of Catholic, Protestant, and Jewish scholars, is a striking instance of this. Much more might be added, but this is enough to show that, even humanly speaking, we have abundant ground for encouragement.*

* The above was written before the appearance of the elaborate and appreciative review of Dr. Newman's *Letter on the Eirenicon* in the *Times* of March 31, which does full justice on the whole to the transcendent powers and lofty character of that 'great writer, of whose genius and religious feeling Englishmen will be one day even prouder than they are now.' But I must enter my most emphatic protest, as a Catholic, against the strange and paradoxical assertion that 'he offers *not the faintest encouragement to Dr. Pusey's sanguine hopes*,' when he pointedly insists on the fact that Dr. Pusey has '*put the whole argument on a new footing*,' and that on the relative authority of Scripture and Tradition—which underlies the entire controversy—' the difference between Catholics and Anglicans *is merely one of words*.' Still I hail the review, as the former review of the *Eirenicon*, with sincere satisfaction, and for the same reason. The prominence given by the *Times* to the leading writers on the Reunion

Above all, I would appeal to the young. *Spes messis in semine.* The hopes of a nation, or of a Church, are centred in its youth. The future lies with them to make or mar. And youth is the age of generous impulse, of chivalrous devotion, of that unworldly wisdom which is not ashamed of enthusiasm in a noble cause. There is no more glorious page in the history of the early Church than that which records the heroism of her Martyr Boys. To what higher end could life be sacrificed than for restoring Christian unity? What holier martyrdom than to die for it? At this brightest season of the world's and the Church's year, when all is bursting into fresh life around us, and the air rings with Alleluias, let us gaze in faith on the renewed miracle of nature's resurrection, and believe that for the supernatural kingdom also there is the promise of a second spring. To the young I appeal—and I know that they will hear me—for to them especially belongs that blessed promise, and on them depends its fulfilment.

Before concluding, I would turn for a moment to those whom I would fain be able to reckon among the friends and not the opponents of this sacred cause, but who seem disposed to take their stand on the isolated and exclusive claims of Established Angli-

question on either side is far more important, as a moral fact, than its carefully guarded intimation of its fear that 'in our time at least' reunion is improbable. That it should be treated as desirable and publicly discussed is a great point gained.

canism as the great palladium of the national religion, the spiritual castle which it is an Englishman's first duty to defend against all comers, the grand bulwark against—to use language which has unhappily become classical—'the corruptions of Popery on the one hand, and the insolence of Dissent on the other.' I will meet them with no arguments of my own. I gladly avail myself at the last moment of the recently published utterances of two writers, differing, I believe, widely in many things from each other and from myself, but equally devoted to the National Church, at whose altars both of them minister, and equally outspoken in their remonstrance against that narrow and sectarian temper which would make it a test of allegiance to her to hold off Christendom at arm's length. It is not the less agreeable to me to be able to appeal to their words, that with one I have the pleasure of a slight acquaintance, while my long standing friendship with the other is consecrated by the undying memories of old Oxford days. The latter, after pointedly asking whether there is 'any reason in the nature of things why the English Church and nation should continue to be what it is—*a microcosm of all the religious differences and disorders of Christendom*'? proceeds to inquire whether 'Nonconformist aggressiveness' is altogether a fair reproach in the mouth of Anglicans. 'Have we done, are we doing, nothing to justify and even stimulate that ambition—to give ground for it to wonder whether it [Nonconformity] *might not one day come to tolerate us?* I submit that there is much to make us pause and reflect in the fact of two-thirds of the community (especially if that be only a polite hypothesis for a much smaller fraction) assuming to tolerate the other third as loftily as we are wont to do.'* Mr. Plumptre, commenting on this same writer in the 'Contemporary Review,' strikes a bolder note. 'I know not whether it will be given to us to get rid of that antipathy of which I have already spoken,—to shake off the inheritance of prejudices, divisions, antagonisms which we have received from our fathers and seem likely to transmit to our children. Notable efforts have been made lately *to cut off this entail of curses*, and to diminish the bitterness which has come between us and the great Churches of the East and West. Such efforts, however imprudent or impracticable they may seem to us, *ought at least to command our respectful sympathy*. We are so accustomed, in thought and act, to take up the spirit of the old proverb, and say that the 'fathers have eaten sour grapes, and the children's teeth are set on edge,'—to throw the blame on the sins of a past generation, *and then to repeat the sins ourselves*,—that it is well when any one rises and speaks as with authority, and bids us know that we ought to have "no more occasion to use that proverb in Israel." '† Such words are but an echo, from what had long been a hostile camp, to those of Möhler,

---

* *The Conscience Clause*, by J. Oakley, M.A., pp. 59, 63.
† *Contemporary Review* for April, p. 602.

Döllinger, Wiseman, of the greatest thinkers and holiest pastors in every age of our divided Christendom. And while they appeal directly to those who are of the writer's communion, to us Catholics they are at once an encouragement and a warning—an encouragement to the hope that God will 'devise a way to bring His banished home,' a warning lest their zeal to seek renewed fellowship with us outstrip our zeal to welcome them.

And let me add that never was there a time when the Church of England had so strong a claim as now on the sympathy and co-operation of Catholics for regaining her rightful position within the sphere of corporate unity. If Cardinal Wiseman considered the 'facilities for reunion' in 1841 greater than *ever* before existed, what shall we say now? In 1857 a Catholic writer observed: 'The National Church *is becoming more vigorous and more influential every day*; there never was a more unpractical or improbable notion than that which, in spite of such facts, would still count upon its destruction, or build airy castles upon its anticipated ruins.'* In 1864 another Catholic says emphatically: 'It is impossible to ignore the Church of England. *She has not been more active for good or stronger for many centuries.* Her words and work are before God and man.'† And they are right. Thirty years

* *The Future Unity of Christendom*, by A. L. Phillipps (De Lisle), p. 16.

† Letter in *Union Review* for May 1864, p. 328, signed 'Catholicus Dunelmensis.'

ago, when her Sees were being suppressed, her Cathedrals threatened, her exclusive privileges torn out of the Statute-book, it seemed to many even of her warmest adherents as though she had nothing to fall back upon, and were losing her hold over the hearts and consciences of her members. But what a moral resurrection our eyes have witnessed since then! Her Cathedrals restored and thrown open for popular services, many thousands of parish churches built or rebuilt up and down the length and breadth of the land, Convocation at work after more than a century's slumber, and already opening negotiations with the Eastern Churches, Diocesan Synods and Church Congresses assembling, some fifty Colonial Sees erected—these are but the outward signs of a spiritual revival such as has never been granted to any other separated communion. Never, I suppose, was preaching more earnest, or the parochial system made more of a reality, or Communions more frequent, or sacred seasons more largely observed, or congregations more numerous and devout, within her pale, than now. Not many years ago it was the fashion even among friendly observers to say that the Church of England was 'dying of dignity.' We have lived to see a Bishop of London lay aside his dignity and go to preach in an omnibus yard to the spiritual outcasts of this huge metropolis. Anglican Sisterhoods, which twenty years ago would have been dismissed, by friend and foe alike, as an idle chimera, have become an established fact, with the full sanction of ecclesiastical authority and of public opinion. Some analogous institution for men who wish to devote themselves to a corporate life of active charity seems to be feeling its way to a recognition. A Church that is everywhere rebuilding her altars and recovering her people cannot be said to be in a state of decrepitude or decay. Whatever be her special mission in the Providence of God, it seems abundantly manifest that some important future is reserved for her, and that, as De Maistre long ago insisted, 'she is very precious' to Christendom. One thing indeed we know, that her mission can never be adequately realised till she is restored to Catholic unity; and one thing we can all of us do, which is to labour and pray, as the late Cardinal bade us, for 'the accomplishment of this noble end.' Duties are ours; the future rests with God.

And now it is time to bring these remarks to a close. I have written under the growing pressure of strong and imperative convictions, not for controversy, but for truth. I have said—and said deliberately—what must displease partizans on every side; but a still small voice is making itself heard amid 'the battle of the Churches,' the din of controversy, and the jarring watchwords of rival sects, which whispers to the inmost conscience of those who will pause to listen, that God is not in the wind, or the earthquake, or the fire, that the wrath of man can never be the instrument of His justice, and that truthfulness and charity are the first conditions of any victory that deserves the name. The wisdom that descends from above is 'peaceable' as well as 'pure;' if the vision of God is promised to the pure in heart, the 'peacemakers' are to be called His children. The bequest of Jesus to His disciples before He suffered was the gift of peace. The 'new commandment,' coincident in origin as in character with the Sacrifice of the new dispensation, is that we 'love one another.' Love is the spirit of the Gospel, of the Church, of the Eucharist; 'love is the fulfilling of the law;' without love even an Apostle is 'nothing.' And what is unity but the outward expression of that love? Let us rise to the greatness of the occasion, the gravity of the interests at stake. There is a yearning for unity among brethren long divided, such as for three long centuries has not been witnessed. The breath of the Lord has gone forth, and there is a shaking of the dry bones as though they would come together again, 'an exceeding great army,' the true Israel of our God. But His call awaits our free response; His gracious work is ours to make or mar. A great opportunity is set before us; let it not be said to-day, as once of old, that He would have gathered His children together, *and we would not*; lest our house be left unto us desolate! Let us take on our lips and grave deeply on our hearts the Church's solemn admonition, *Sursum corda*! Let us cast away, as an accursed thing, the bitterness of party spirit, the blindness of prejudice, the ignorance of malice, the selfishness of spiritual pride, the godless traditions of three bitter centuries of strife. 'A great door is opened to us, as says the Apostle St. Paul, and our first duty is *not to close it* by excess of zeal, of severity, or of any other blameable sentiment. *To pray God that He will accomplish the work begun is another duty, from which no one should hold aloof.'*

This last suggestion of the learned Jesuit had been more than anticipated in the earnest and impressive words of the illustrious Bishop Ketteler of Mayence, in the work already referred to; ' What would above all rejoice us would be to see members of the different Christian communions deliberate together *on the organisation of a prayer to be recited in common by all who believe in the true divinity of Jesus Christ.* We do not think God *could possibly fail to hear a prayer* by which we should beseech Him that we may all form one body, *ut omnes unum sint.*'† It may well be hoped that this call to united prayer is one which believing Christians on every side will not reject. I do not ask them to join this or that particular Association or Confraternity; I do not wish them to pray for anything they do not themselves believe in. But I do ask them to pray—in whatever form or manner their consciences may most approve—that the Prayer of Jesus may be fulfilled on earth—that all who are sealed with His Baptism, and bear His

---

* *Études Religieuses*, No. 37, p. 134, quoted by Dr. Pusey in letter to *Guardian* of Jan. 24.

† *Liberté, Autorité, Église*, p. 230.

Name, may be gathered round the altars of a common worship, and own a common faith. To my Catholic readers I would say further, our late Cardinal Archbishop 'being dead yet speaketh' in the closing words of his earnest plea for unity: 'In one point I trust that none (however he may have differed with me so far) will refuse to join me—*in daily and fervent supplication to the God of peace that He will deign to direct our hearts and conduct towards the accomplishment of this noble end.*'* Elsewhere I have said something of other ways in which all, the least as well as the greatest, may contribute to the same object, and I need not repeat it here.† But it was impossible to omit all reference to that paramount obligation, which is also our glorious privilege, of uniting our poor intercessions with those of the Church Universal—Militant, Suffering, Triumphant—that He who bequeathed to His Apostles the gift of peace, would 'not regard our offences, but His Church's faith, and vouchsafe to her that peace and unity which is according to His blessed will.' For He has made our prayers the law of His Providence, and the condition of His gifts.

One word more, and I have done. It has been for years my deep and irrepressible conviction, that it is as really—though for different reasons and in different degrees—the common and urgent interest of all alike who are now so unhappily divided, that

---

* *Letter to Lord Shrewsbury*, pp. 41, 42.
† See *Sermons on Reunion*, vol. i. Serm. V; vol. ii. Serm. II.

the wounds of Christendom should be healed; and more particularly, speaking as an Englishman, that those two great Communions which stand face to face in this our own dear country should again, as of old, be one. What I said as an Anglican I may repeat now as a Catholic: 'One thing at least is clear. If the predicted struggle against the "Lawless One"—him who is described by St. John as "the spirit that dissolveth Jesus"—be indeed coming upon us (and there is certainly much in the present aspect of the civilized world which *looks* as though such a day were approaching), nothing short of a united Church [I meant a united Christendom] can be equal to the crisis.'* What I said then of the rival Churches I feel as keenly now; that *we want them, and they want us.* They want us, if they will permit me to say so (and I speak not now of any points in controversy between us), in order to gain that firmer and more authoritative grasp of dogmatic truth, that clearer appreciation of theological principles, that deeper acquaintance with the spiritual and ascetic life, and that more elastic and successful organisation of missionary enterprise, whether foreign or domestic, the fruit of self-crucified charity, which have their human basis in the characteristics of the Latin race, and their divine consecration in the unity and sanctity of the Church of God. And we want them, that we may learn to emulate that larger toleration, that more searching and accurate criti-

* *Church Parties*, Preface, pp. ix. x.

G

cism, that stubborn love of truth for its own sake, in which Catholics have sometimes allowed themselves to be surpassed by their alienated brethren; in order, in a word, that we may recover and reconsecrate for the service of the Church the restless energy, the indomitable will, the strong practical sense, the natural instinct of religious reverence, which are among the noblest endowments of the great Anglo-Saxon race. We want each other, that the diverse but harmonious elements of moral, intellectual, and spiritual life which have for three long centuries been held apart in an unnatural divorce may be once more wedded in a sacred and indissoluble union; that what is tenderest, and purest, and holiest in the order of nature may be in accord, and not in antagonism, with what is akin to it in the supernatural order of grace. Then, and not till then, shall those words of ancient prophecy, which ring almost like a mockery in our ears, receive their adequate fulfilment. Then indeed shall the glory of the Lord arise upon His holy City, the New Jerusalem that came down out of heaven from God, and kings shall walk in her light, and nations in the brightness of her shining; Ephraim shall no more envy Judah, nor Judah vex Ephraim, but the knowledge of the True God and of Jesus whom He hath sent, which is life eternal, shall cover the earth, as the waters cover the sea!

For this thousands are daily interceding; for this it were well to devote the energies, to sacrifice the happiness of a lifetime. May He, the All-merciful

Redeemer, vouchsafe in His own good time to grant our prayers, and if it be His blessed will, so that our eyes may see it! May He touch the hearts, and utterly confound and bring to nought, as though they had never been, the schemes, the hopes, and the endeavours of all who through mistaken zeal would thwart His gracious purpose! And meanwhile may He bestow His richest and most varied benedictions on all, wherever found, who, whether by their sympathies, their energies, or their prayers, have contributed—though it be but as a cup of cold water given in His name, or a mite cast into His treasury—towards an object so dear to His Sacred Heart, which formed the burden of His great Eucharistic intercession the night before He suffered, which from that day to this has been continually remembered in the Canon of every Mass!

O Clavis David, et Sceptrum domûs Israel, QUI APERIS ET NEMO CLAUDIT, *claudis et nemo aperit; O Oriens Splendor Lucis Æternæ, et Sol Justitiæ, veni, et illumina sedentes in tenebris et in umbra mortis! O Rex Gentium et Desideratus earum,* LAPISQUE ANGULARIS QUI FACIS UTRAQUE UNUM; *O Emmanuel, Rex et Legifer noster, Expectatio Gentium et Salvator earum; veni ad salvandum nos, Domine Deus noster!*

Ever, my dear Father Lockhart,

Affectionately yours,

H. N. OXENHAM.

Easter Eve, 1866.

APPENDIX.

TESTIMONIES OF CATHOLIC, GREEK, AND ANGLICAN WRITERS TO THE IMPORTANCE AND DUTY OF REUNION.

I PROPOSE to insert in this Appendix extracts from the works of Catholic, Oriental, and Anglican writers on the importance of visible unity. All are men of name and position in their respective communions and countries, and of the present century; nor would it have been difficult to swell the list by adding the testimony of honoured though less illustrious witnesses to the same great principle. It will of course be readily understood that they approach the question from very various points of view, according to their differences of antecedents or belief, and that the agreement between them is to be sought in a common aim, not in a uniform conception of the right methods for attaining it. I have tried to select such passages as were least suggestive of controversy, but without thinking it necessary always to exclude what could not be quoted with entire satisfaction, where it gave important evidence to the writer's general desire for restoration of visible unity among Christians. The authorities collected here will at least be sufficient to prove that Dr. Pusey cannot be regarded as a solitary enthusiast for suggesting what many of the best and wisest both of his communion and of ours have so persuasively urged before him. They will show further that the yearning for restored brotherhood among all who name the Name of Christ is not confined to any one national or religious division of Christendom. I shall begin with Catholic writers, and proceed to those of the Oriental and Anglican Churches, taking the documents in chronological order, except that in each case the testimony of an eminent layman will close the list. For the reader's convenience it may be well to prefix the names of the writers about to be quoted:—

Catholic Writers.

Bishop Doyle.
Möhler.
Cardinal Wiseman.
Bishop of Mayence.

Döllinger.
Bishop of Orleans.
Phillipps de Lisle.

Writers of the Greek Church.

Patriarch of Constantinople.
Archbishop of Belgrade.
Archbishop of Corcyra.

Bishop of Ephesus.
Prince Orloff.

Anglican Writers.

Bishop Barrington.
Bishop of Brechin.
Bishop of Salisbury.
Bishop of Capetown.

Bennett.
Carter.
Gladstone.

BISHOP DOYLE.

Dr. Doyle, the late Bishop of Kildare and Leighlin, who was at the time quite the leading member of the Irish Catholic Episcopate, addressed a letter in 1824 to the then Chancellor of the Exchequer (afterwards Lord Ripon), which, as being written before the commencement of the Oxford movement, and with special reference to the Established Church of *Ireland*, has an *à fortiori* application to the circumstances of our own day, and of this country. It was published in the newspapers, and was favourably noticed at the time by Archbishop Murray, as by many others, both Catholics and Protestants. A digest of its contents, with long extracts, is given in Fitzpatrick's 'Life, Times, and Correspondence of Dr. Doyle' (Duffy, 1861) vol. i. pp. 421–423.

'The union of the Churches, which you have had the singular merit of suggesting to the Commons of the United Kingdom, would at once effect a total change in the dispositions of men;

it would bring all classes to co-operate zealously in promoting the prosperity of Ireland, and in securing her allegiance for ever to the British Throne. . . . *This union, on which so much depends, is not, as you have justly observed, so difficult as appears to many*; and the present time is peculiarly well calculated for attempting, at least, to carry it into effect. It is not difficult, for in the discussions which were held, and the correspondence which occurred on this subject early in the last century, as well as that in which Archbishop Tillotson was engaged, and the others which were carried on between Bossuet and Leibnitz, it appeared that *the points of agreement between the Churches were numerous, those on which the parties hesitated few, and apparently not the most important.* The effort which was then made was not attended with success, but *its failure was owing more to Princes than to Priests, more to State policy than to a difference of belief.* But the same reasons which at that period disappointed the hopes of every good Christian in Europe would at present operate favourably. For what interest can England *now* have which is opposed to such a Union? and what nation or Church in the universe can have stronger motives for desiring it than Great Britain, if by it she could preserve her Church Establishment, perfect her internal policy, and secure her external dominion? . . . . It may not become so humble an individual as I am, to hint even at a plan for effecting so great a purpose as the union of Catholics and Protestants in one great family of Christians; but as the difficulty does not appear to me to be at all proportioned to the magnitude of the object to be attained, I would presume to state, that if Protestant and Catholic Divines of learning, and a conciliatory character, were summoned by the Crown to ascertain the points of agreement and difference between the Churches, and the result of their conferences were made the basis of a project to be treated on between the heads of the Church of Rome and of England, the result might be more favourable than at present would be anticipated. The chief points to be discussed are the Canon of the Sacred Scriptures, Faith, Justification, the Mass, the Sacraments, the Authority of Tradition, of Councils, of the Pope, the Celibacy of the Clergy, Language of the Liturgy, Invocation of Saints, Respect for Images, Prayers for the Dead. *On most of these, it appears to me that there is no essential difference between the Catholics and Protestants*; the existing diversity of opinion arises, in most cases, from certain *forms of words* which admit of satisfactory explanation, or from *the ignorance or misconceptions* which ancient prejudice and ill-will produce and strengthen, but which could be removed; they are pride and points of honour, which keep us divided on many subjects, not a love of Christian humility, charity, and truth.'

MÖHLER.

Möhler's principal work, the 'Symbolism,' from which the following extract is taken, was originally published in 1832, when he was Professor of Dogmatic Theology in the Catholic Faculty of Tübingen; at a period, therefore, when such sentiments as are here expressed were less common than now, and when there was very little in the religious phenomena of the day to suggest them. Cardinal Wiseman comments on the following passage in his Letter to Lord Shrewsbury (p. 33), as corroborating his own views, and expressing 'the feeling of the profound and pious Möhler,' and quotes in italics (from the French translation) the portion of it which I have also italicised here. I give it as it stands in Robertson's English Translation, vol. ii. pp. 31, 32:—

'The Protestants themselves furnish an irrefragable proof of the state of manifold neglect into which the people had fallen during the fifteenth century. Never would a system of doctrine like theirs have sprung up, still less have obtained such wide diffusion, had individual teachers and priests been faithful to the duties of their calling. Truly, the ignorance could not have been slight, on which a system of faith, like that of the Reformers, was imposed as worthy of acceptance; and thus Protestants may learn to estimate the magnitude of the evil, which then oppressed the Church, by the magnitude of the errors into which they themselves have fallen. *This is the point at which Catholics and Protestants will, in great multitudes, one day meet, and stretch a friendly hand one to the other. Both, conscious of guilt, must exclaim,* " *We all have erred, it is the Church only which cannot err; we have all sinned, the Church only is spotless on earth.*" This open confession of mutual guilt will be followed by the festival of reconciliation. Meanwhile, we still smart under the inexpressible pain of the wound which was then inflicted—a pain which can be alleviated only by the consciousness that the wound has become an issue, through which all the impurities have flowed off which men had introduced into the wide compass of the dominions of the Church; for she herself is ever pure and eternally undefiled.'

CARDINAL WISEMAN.

The 'Letter to Lord Shrewsbury,' which I have so frequently had occasion to refer to in the foregoing pages, appeared in the autumn of 1841, about six months after the publication of Tract 90, which seems to have more immediately suggested it. The date is important, when we remember how strongly the author insists, in considerable detail, on the 'facilities for the reunion of England to the Catholic Church *beyond what have before existed*, and particularly under Archbishop Laud, or Wake' (p. 35); and that he records his deliberate conviction 'that no one who has the means of judging can doubt that the feelings which have been expressed, in favour of *a return to unity by the Anglican Church*, are every day widely spreading and deeply sinking.' Such words come to us now, after the lapse of a quarter of a century, with a greatly accumulated evidence and force.

'I am sure your Lordship will agree with me that the very attempt to heal the religious sores of this noble country would immortalise any minister who should undertake it. May I not add, that the neglect of this great moral plague is enough, in the end to frustrate every other effort to cure its evils? . . . The idea of all England's being, in religion, one, is incompatible with her remaining in her present state of ecclesiastical and religious isolation, as under the rule of a 'national' Church, in the invidious sense of the word, *that is, separated from the religious communion of the rest of the world*. We Catholics must necessarily deplore the separation as a deep moral evil; as a state of schism of which nothing can justify the continuance. Many members of the Anglican Church view it in the same light as to the first point—its sad evil; though they excuse their individual position in it as an unavoidable misfortune. Many of us, therefore, are in accordance thus far, that the sooner an end can be put to the present painful position of the Anglican Church, with relation to the rest of the world, the better; and we may depend upon a willing, an able, and a most zealous co-operation with any effort we may make *towards bringing her into her rightful position*, in Catholic unity with the Holy See and the Churches of its obedience—in other words, with the Church Catholic. Is this a visionary idea? is it merely the expression of a strong desire? *I know that many will so judge it;* and perhaps were I to consult my own quiet, I would not venture to express it. But I will, in simplicity of heart, cling to hopefulness, cheered, as I feel it, by so many promising appearances. . . . That the return of this country (*through its Established Church*) to the Catholic unity would put an end to religious dissent and interior feud, I feel no doubt. By two ways the population of the country would be worked on for its moral improvement—the rural districts through parochial influence, the denser population of towns or manufacturing districts through the monastic institutions. Experience has now shown that the country population are ready to receive without murmuring, indeed with pleasure, the Catholic views propounded from Oxford, and indeed even more, *when taught through regular parochial instruction*. Add the richness and majesty of the Catholic Ritual, the variety of its sublime services, the touching offices of peculiar seasons, the numberless institutions for charitable objects, and its hourly sanctifications of domestic life, *and dissent would break in pieces beneath the silent action of universal attraction*, and its fragments gather round its all-powerful principle. . . . *In one point I trust that none* (however he may have differed with me so far) *will refuse to join me*—in daily and fervent supplication to the God of peace, that He will deign to direct our hearts and conduct towards the accomplishment of this noble end. *Let us interest the entire Church in our favour;* the surest pledge which we can have that God intends to grant a blessing, is His inspiring His spouse to entreat Him. The golden sceptre will be stretched out to her the moment she goes to pray for "her own soul and for her people."' (Pp. 6, 11, 40-42.)

When we read in 1866 these words penned by the Cardinal in

1841, does not much that is passing before our eyes to-day look almost like the fulfilment of a prophecy? It may at least encourage us to enter into the spirit of his admonition, in the Sermon on Religious Unity, in a volume published the year before his death, 'not to brood over past judgments, but turn rather to the future with hope,' striving to 'be again, as the first Christians were, firmly united in one faith, and we shall soon be as they, possessed of one heart.' The whole Letter, from which my extracts are taken, deserves careful perusal.

BISHOP OF MAYENCE.

The following noble passage is from a work published in 1862 by the present Bishop of Mayence, Ketteler, who was formerly one of Dr. Döllinger's most distinguished pupils at Munich, and is no less conspicuous among the German Episcopate by his ability, than by his position as occupant, by special selection of the Holy See in 1848, of one of its most important Sees, formerly a Prince Bishopric and seat of an Elector of the Holy Roman Empire. I quote from the French translation of 'Liberté, Autorité, Église,' published with the author's sanction, not having had an opportunity of consulting the original. The passage will be found at p. 227, sqq. :—

'The greater part of mankind, disdaining the Divine assistance, preferred darkness to light. They crucified Christ, and the evil spirit which accomplished that crime has never ceased to attack and persecute His Church. Not content with hindering to the utmost of its power the diffusion among men of the rich treasures of Divine love and compassion, it *has even rent asunder the bosom of Christianity, and sown division among the members of the body of Jesus Christ.* Hence the unhappy rupture between the Churches of East and West, *which still continues to thwart the mission of Christianity.* Hence the no less deplorable division in the Catholic Church in the West, *which for three centuries has preyed on our vitals, and is the source of such deadly mischief.* Hence the numberless divisions among Protestants themselves, feebly restrained by the influence of the civil power. Hence, lastly, the new enemy, Deism, which has appeared in the world, and struggles against Christianity in the very bosom of Christendom. First, it denied supernatural revelation, i. e. all intercourse between God and man, except what is founded on nature and unassisted natural reason. This was to deny the Divinity of Christ and of His work. He was no longer the Wisdom that dwelt before the throne of God, and came down from heaven to humble Himself to man's estate. After denying Divine revelation, Deism denied the supernatural order, and, finally, any God above nature. This is our present foe; and serious minds, like the Protestant M. Guizot, divide mankind into two camps, those who believe in a personal God, and those who do not. All really Christian hearts are profoundly grieved at so sad a state of things, and in view of the divisions which devastate Christendom. They perceive that the unexampled abomination, witnessed eighteen centuries after the appearance of the Son of God on earth, of fools who say not only in their heart but in their public teaching, "There is no God,"* *springs wholly from these dissensions.* Catholics ought to share this feeling of sorrow to the very bottom of their hearts. How different is the present aspect of Christendom from that Jesus Christ prayed for, "That they may be one, even as We are One."† *It is our duty to strive to the very utmost to restore this union. No Catholic, however small his power, should refuse his help.* The humblest materials are employed in the grandest buildings. But there are two chief means which, in my opinion, we can all use. *The first is to pray for the reunion of all the Christian confessions.* Would that this unanimous prayer could be organised on a common plan, accepted by all the Christian souls which long for the reunion of the various religious societies! Christ attached the most glorious promises to united prayer, saying, that whatever we asked the Father in His Name should be done. What would not be the efficacy of our prayer, if we all united with our great High Priest in His last earthly prayer, "that they may be one, as Thou Father in Me, and I in Thee," *ut omnes unum sint*! Of late this thought has deeply moved men's minds; may its influence increase, and find an increasing response and sympathy! *We conjure all sincere Christians, who adopt this expression of their feeling, to make themselves its apostles, and spread it among their*

---

* Psalm xiii. 1. † John xvii. 22.

friends. Some eminent men have tried to promote the same object by conferences. But, while rejoicing in these attempts, we doubt, to say the truth, whether God will bless them with any signal success. What would still more rejoice us would be *to see men of different Christian communions deliberate together for organising the recital of some common prayer by all who believe that Jesus Christ is the true and only Son of God.* I cannot think that God could refuse to hear a prayer that we should for the future form but one body, *ut omnes unum sint.** The second means for procuring reunion depends on us Catholics. It consists in avoiding every sort of scandal, and displaying in our conduct the great supernatural virtues of Christianity. Nothing so much repels men who are well disposed from Catholic truths, as seeing them obscured, as it were, and hidden from the world by the vices of children of our Church. *Nearly all the reproaches urged against the Catholic Church are based on misapprehensions, and these almost always have their source in the imperfections and infirmities of members of the Church.* . . . At the same time, great as is our desire for the reunion of all Christian bodies, we Catholics must not conceal that we recognise no centre of unity but the Roman Church. The Catholic Church is based on two fundamental principles, which distinguish it from every other body, and to which recent events give a fresh confirmation. *The first* is, that we are united to Christ by an external bond, consisting in *the uninterrupted succession of the apostolate.*' His Lordship then dwells for some pages on the apostolic succession, the priesthood, and the sacraments, saying nothing which Anglican High Churchmen would not readily accept. He then proceeds : ' The *second* fundamental principle of the Church is, *the existence of a teaching* authority, which, by virtue of assistance from above, cannot be deceived in interpreting *the doctrine of Jesus Christ.* Contrary to the Protestant view, that we only know the word of God from Scripture, Catholicism affirms that it is chiefly

---

* In 1853 a society was established at Rome, under Papal sanction, called 'The Eastern Christian Society,' for the purpose of reuniting Christendom, 'first by restoring unity between the Eastern and Western Churches;' and secondly, 'by bringing the Protestant communities into fellowship with the main body of the Church.' See *Future Unity of Christendom,* pp. 32, 33, quoting Pitzipios.

transmitted through the teaching ministry.' He proceeds to contrast the two principles of authoritative Tradition and the Bible only, in precisely the sense of a passage in the 'Christian Remembrancer.' 'We mean by the principle of Protestantism, of course, Scripture as interpreted by individuals; by that of Catholicism, we mean adherence to what the Church, when adequately represented, has defined, however little it may appear on the surface of Scripture.'* The Bishop concludes with the following explanation: 'To preclude misapprehensions, I will repeat what I have said elsewhere; the infallible authority of the teaching Church *only extends to truths proclaimed by Christ*; it does not reside immediately in each separate Bishop, but only *in the whole body of the Episcopate, united to the successor of St. Peter*. A Bishop who separates himself from this centre, removes from the stream of living truth which emanates from Christ, and fills the whole body of the Church.'

DÖLLINGER.

There are few of Dr. Döllinger's recent publications in which the supreme importance of a reunion of the divided confessions does not hold a prominent place. The following extracts are given in the chronological order of the appearance of the works they are derived from, ranging from 1861 to 1864. The first is from 'The Church and the Churches,' published in Germany in 1861, and in an English Translation in the following year, when it attracted considerable attention, and formed the subject of articles in the 'Edinburgh' and several other Reviews in this country. I quote from the English Translation, Introd., pp. 16–19.

'Upon the day when, on both sides, the conviction shall arise, vivid and strong, that Christ really desires the unity of His Church, *that the division of Christendom, the multiplicity of Churches, is displeasing to God*—that he who helps to prolong this situation must answer for it to the Lord—on that day four-fifths of the traditional polemics of Protestants against the Catholic Church will, with one blow, be cast aside like chaff and rubbish; for four-fifths of it consists of misunderstandings, logomachies, and

* *Chr. Rem.*, Jan. 1866, p 167.

wilful falsifications; or relate to personal, and therefore accidental, things, which are utterly insignificant, where only principles and dogmas are at stake. On that day also much will be changed on the Catholic side. . . . We do not refuse to admit that the great separation, and the storms and sufferings connected with it, were an awful judgment upon Catholic Christendom, which clergy and laity had but too well deserved—a judgment which has had an improving and salutary effect. The great intellectual conflict has purified the European atmosphere, has impelled the human mind on to new courses, and has promoted a rich scientific and literary life. Protestant theology, with its restless spirit of inquiry, has gone along by the side of the Catholic, exciting and awakening, warming and vivifying; whilst every exalted Catholic theologian will readily admit that he owes much to the writings of Protestant scholars. We have also to own that in the Church the rust of abuses, and of a mechanical superstition, is always forming afresh; that the servants of the Church sometimes, through indolence and incapacity, and the people through ignorance, brutify the spiritual in religion, and thus degrade and deform and misemploy it to their own injury. *The right reforming spirit must therefore never depart from the Church*, but, on the contrary, must periodically break out with renovating strength, and penetrate the conscience and the will of the clergy. . . . And yet it must never be forgotten that the separation did not ensue in consequence of abuses in the Church. . . . It was for the sake of *doctrine* that the separation occurred; and the general discontent of the people, the weakening of ecclesiastical authority by the existence of abuses, only facilitated the adoption of the new doctrines. But now, upon the one side, some of these defects and evils in the life of the Church have disappeared, and more have greatly diminished since the reforming movement. And, on the other side, *the principal doctrines for which men separated*, and on the truth of which, and their necessity for salvation, the right and duty of secession had been based, *are given up by Protestant science*, deprived of their Scriptural basis by exegesis, or, at least, made very uncertain by the opposition of the most eminent Protestant theologians. Meanwhile we live in hope; comforting ourselves with the conviction that history, or *that process of de-*

velopment in Europe which is being accomplished before our eyes (as well in science and politics as in religion), *is the powerful ally of the friends of ecclesiastical union* ; and we hold out our hands to Christians on the other side for a combined war of resistance against the destructive movements of the age. For this, to use the words of Von Radowitz, is the state of affairs: " We plainly perceive that the minds of men are ranging themselves under two banners, upon one of which is inscribed the name of ' Christ, the Son of God,' and beneath the other are incorporated all to whom that Name is foolishness and a reproach." '

The next extract is from the Speech delivered by Dr. Döllinger at the opening of the Munich Congress, Sept. 28, 1863, and published in the report of its proceedings (' Verhandlungen der Versammlung katholischer Gelehrten in München,' 1863; and separately under the title of ' Rede über Vergangenheit und Gegenwart der katholischen Theologie '). It occurs at pp. 45–47 of the former, pp. 20–22 of the latter. Unfortunately, no English translation of the Speech has as yet appeared. The speaker was of course referring immediately to the religious condition of his own country, but the general application of his words is obvious on the surface. A few lines are omitted, bearing on the special capabilities of German Theology for subserving the cause of union.

' It is our peculiarity, among all nations, that the sharp iron of ecclesiastical division has pierced us through and through, and split us into two almost equal halves, which can neither part from each other nor live together. Two halves, I say, which at the bottom of their heart long for union, since they feel the curse of this division at every step, and in every pulsation of national life; which at once love and hate one another, make war and stretch out the hand of brotherhood. It is this which has cast a dark shadow over our history. We are sick, as a nation, like Philoctetes, from the running sore of the poisoned arrow. To many the wound appears incurable, nor has anyone as yet been able to name a remedy. Yet our endeavours after a better political constitution are labour lost till it is cured. This is self-evident to every thinking man. Only four days ago our most widely read newspaper said plainly : " *German unity is the union of the Confessions in Germany.*"* We should be constrained to despair

---

* *Allgemeine Zeitung*, Sept. 24, 1863.

of ourselves and our future, if we lost our faith in the possibility, nay certainty, of religious union—that it is no less certain than the strong enduring vitality of the German people, or the promise that the gates of Hell shall not prevail against the Church. . . . . The first condition [of union] is, that our [theological] science, using those means now more than ever at its command, should overcome all that is really uncatholic and tending to division in the teaching of the opposite side—all, that is, *which contradicts the common consciousness of the Church of all ages, and the continuity of tradition*; and this is far from being accomplished yet. The second condition is, that it should exhibit Catholic doctrine, as a whole, in its connection with the Church's life, its organic coherence and internal sequence, and should at the same time *sharply distinguish what is essential and permanent from what is accidental and temporary, or an excrescence foreign to the original idea.* This has by no means been done yet, and a sincere answer to the question, why it has not been done, would be a contribution to that self-knowledge so needful and so wholesome for us. Finally, the third condition would be, that Theology, and through it the Church, should gain the nature and power of the magnetic mountain in the story, which drew out all the iron from the ships that came near, so that they fell to pieces; I mean that she should carefully distinguish from its admixture of error whatever of goodness the separated communions have discovered or originated, in doctrine, history, and life, and then freely and openly accept it, nay claim it, as the rightful property of the One True Church, which once possessed all this at least in germ and outline. Error only lives by virtue of those grains of truth which it contains, and is often only the caricature of a hidden truth. I said publicly two years ago, that now and in the immediate future, union was not possible, because the majority of Protestants did not wish for it. I would fain have added that on our side it was all the more earnestly desired and striven after. But truth and justice forbade me then, and forbid me to-day to say so. *For he alone wills an end who wills the means without which it is unattainable, and shows his will by his acts.* And the means in this case are humility, brotherly love, self-denial, *hearty recognition of the good and true, wherever found*, a profound appreciation of the defects, evils, and scandals of our own condition, and an earnest will to labour for their removal.'

My third and last extract is taken from an Address delivered by Dr. Döllinger before the Scientific Academy of Munich, March 30, 1864, on the occasion of the death of its founder, King Maximilian II. of Bavaria, and published under the title of 'König Maximilian II. und Wissenschaft.' The speaker is recording the sentiments of his royal master and friend, but so as to imply his own agreement with them. The earnestness and hopeful confidence of his tone in discussing, and almost predicting, the reunion of Catholics and Protestants in Germany, may remind us of Bossuet's zealous endeavours for a similar object under less favourable circumstances,* while it is strikingly suggestive of encouragement to ourselves, in a country where the national Church has so much more in common with Catholicism than the 'Evangelical Church' of Germany. The following passage, or portions of it, appeared at the time, I believe, in some of our English papers and periodicals,† but that is no reason why it should not be inserted here. It extends, with the omission of a paragraph of exclusively local interest, from p. 31 to p. 35 of the original.

'The King, as a sincere Christian, had no misgivings about the future permanence of Christianity, and therefore could not believe that the great schism and the battle of the Christian Confessions was to last for ever without hope of remedy, or that noble powers would always be wasted on mutual injury. He thought that God had suffered the separation to last its time, for some higher ends. But now that time had nearly, if not quite, run its course; and he therefore felt convinced that, in spite of all polemical bitterness, all intermixture of impure self-seeking, and the political interests which make capital out of these divisions, a day of union was approaching for the Christian nations, when the promise of One Shepherd and one fold would obtain its perfect fulfilment. For if once the ecclesiastical bodies of the West were united, and brought to bear on the Russo-Greek Church that more than double measure of spiritual power

---

* See *Letter to Lord Shrewsbury*, p. 12.

† To the best of my recollection, in the *Edinburgh, Union Review, Times,* and *Guardian*; perhaps elsewhere also.

which union gives, she would not long resist the overwhelming force of the magnetic attraction to unity. Or if, on the other hand, the Catholic and the Eastern Church were first united, the Protestant bodies would gradually be drawn into the stream of unity. But he looked chiefly, as was natural, to all that more or less directly concerned, or seemed to foreshadow, the peace and reconciliation of Churches in the West, especially in Germany. He saw clearly that the future union *could not be expected to take the form of a simple, unconditional, and as it were mechanical annexation of the separated bodies to each other; nor, again, could a mere absorption of one Church by the other be thought of.* He believed that there must first be a purifying process on both sides, *and that the way must be prepared by the confession that each of the two communions, though in unequal measure, has something to gain from the other, that each wants the help of the other to free it from faults and onesidedness, to fill up gaps in its religious and ecclesiastical life, and to heal its wounds; and that neither must be asked to sacrifice anything proved by living experience to be a real blessing.* Under these conditions the process of reconciliation would sooner or later come to pass in Germany, which is the heart of Europe. . . . He believed that science, especially historical science, had all the more a preparatory mission to discharge here, since religion is itself history, and can only be understood and appreciated as an historical fact, and in accordance with the laws of historical knowledge. He regarded historical science as the kingdom where, in the words of Scripture, righteousness and peace embrace each other; for history, thoroughly investigated and rightly understood, does what nothing else can do—it makes men just in their judgment of their own past and their neighbours', of their own and their neighbours' merits and defects, and thus generates a peaceful and conciliatory disposition. The domain of historical science appeared, then, to the King like the truce of God in the middle ages, or like a consecrated place, where those otherwise divided in religion can meet and carry on their labours and investigations in union with one another; where all, equally thirsting for knowledge and drinking from the same sacred fount of truth, grow into a common fellowship. And he hoped that one day, when the hard ice of confessional antipathies thaws and melts away under a milder atmosphere, there would spring out of this fellowship and brotherhood of science a higher unity, embracing the whole domain of historical, and therefore of religious, truth, and a reconciliation which the patriot and Christian longs and prays for.'

THE BISHOP OF ORLEANS.

The Bishop of Orleans' (Dupanloup's) treatise ('La Convention et l'Encyclique,' 1865), from the 26th edition of which (pp. 126-7) I translate the following apposite passage, received the special approbation of the Pope, and is probably familiar to most of my readers:—

'The ideal of the Pope and of the Church is not anarchy but harmony of intelligences, not the division but the unity of souls. It is that admirable saying of Jesus Christ, "THAT THEY MAY BE ONE," one only flock, one only Shepherd. The unity of minds by the truth, and of hearts by love, is the ideal of the Pope and of the Church. And I venture to add, to the honour of many of my contemporaries, that these aspirations of the Church are shared also by our separated brethren, by the noblest spirits, the best and greatest souls! Men are weary of division; they see no result but sterility and strife. They are weary of this anarchy, *which is the most active solvent of all faith and religious belief*, and the cause of our weakness and incapacity for converting so many idolatrous nations to truth, virtue, and Christian civilisation. What would not be our power for preaching them the Gospel, if we were all agreed. *The majority of mankind are still buried in darkness, because we bring them a disputed, divided, fragmentary Gospel!* Oh! if England, France, and Russia were agreed in the truth, and therefore in apostolic charity and zeal, the face of the East, of the whole world, would be changed. Religious unity! You tell me it is the past, and I reply, from my inmost soul, *that it is the future*, for it is the safety and the honour of the world!'

PHILLIPPS DE LISLE.

To these testimonies of distinguished Catholic Prelates and Ecclesiastics shall be added that of a Layman, whose lifelong labours in the cause of Christian unity, no less than his zeal and munificence in acts of charity, give him a special claim on the respectful attention of all English Catholics. The Essay *On the Future Unity of Christendom*, from which I quote, first published in 1857, should be carefully studied by all who are interested in the question which it handles with no less discrimination than ability. Subsequent events have only increased the force of the writer's argument. A few extracts are all that can be given here, but they should be taken as specimens of the rest, not as substitutes for it. My extracts range from the 6th to the 66th page of the Essay:—

'Roman Catholics, Greeks, and Anglicans, all profess to hold one and the same rule of faith ; and yet the deplorable fact subsists notwithstanding, that these three great communities of Christendom' are more or less severed one from the other, and while they each believe in the same Founder, and each claim authority from Him in virtue of either real or assumed Apostolical descent, so far from acting together in their respective endeavours to carry out our Lord's commission, they are, alas ! in a state of downright antagonism one to the other; instead of concurring together to preach the Gospel to those heathen nations that still reject it, *their time for the most part is consumed in violent controversies among themselves ;* and the result is, that Christians, in the multiplied perplexities of polemical discussions, *are driven from the study of their own individual sanctification*, while the infidel and the sceptic draw forth a plausible argument for their respective blasphemies and doubts. And what is the issue ? Christian nations are far from that actual superiority over nations that are not Christian, in morality and general conduct, which the sublime theory of their religion would have enabled them to attain had it been faithfully carried out. . . . If the State should throw its influence into the scale of the movement, *as one day it infallibly will*, then may the friends of peace and goodwill, of unity and concord, of harmonious and wise legislation, of consequent prosperity and happiness, lift up their heads, for their redemption draweth nigh. The dark night of strife and discord, of hatred and bloodshed, of wickedness and ignorance, will begin to disappear, and the bright rays of truth and justice will beam upon mankind, and England may yet learn, that if God has given her an empire over countless nations and tribes, if He has poured into her lap all the riches of the earth, and raised her to a pitch of glory and power and magnificence, such as no other people has ever attained to, she may yet learn that she has something great to do for God in return for all this, and that this work cannot be achieved by following *a principle of division*, but by carrying out the blessed theory, which in her darkest hour she never entirely abandoned, that theory of Catholic unity and of adherence to the great œcumenical teaching, which has been the result of the commission to " *teach all nations*," entrusted eighteen hundred years ago by Christ our Lord to twelve poor unlearned Jews. Yes, I believe it will be so; and I believe it, not because I hope it, but because *I see* it coming. *Let only Catholics co-operate with their Anglican brethren*, and Anglicans co-operate with Catholics, for the restoration of mutual and corporate unity, for the triumph of Catholic truth, not for the destruction of anything that men hold and cling to as the outward and living form of their visible existence; and the glorious result which every good man must wish for, and which none but evil men would deprecate, will soon crown our mutual and combined efforts. . . . With a theory that so closely approximates to that of Catholic orthodoxy; with a liturgy drawn exclusively from Catholic sources; with a Catechism capable of imbuing the minds of her children with the most Catholic and devout apprehension of the two principal Sacraments—Baptism and the Holy Eucharist; with a ritual containing, if not under the name of Sacraments, yet as rites conveying grace, and the same graces attributed to them by the Catholic theory, the other five Sacraments of the new law, Confirmation, Priestly Absolution, Matrimony, Holy Order, and Extreme Unction—for it would appear that even the last-mentioned rite was retained by King Edward's first Prayer Book, while there is evidence that it has never been wholly abandoned by the orthodox party in the Church of England, at least in theory; . . . I say, with all these badges of Catholicism still preserved by the national Established Church, is there no hope for her ultimate reunion with the rest of Christendom? . . . It is perfectly obvious to any observer of what is going on in England, and what has been now steadily working for twenty-five years, that whatever be the numbers of those who still adhere to ultra-Protestant principles, it is not they who are on the increase in the ranks of the Anglican clergy. On the contrary, it is a fact that very many of the most advanced High Churchmen once belonged to the Evangelical school, or were born of those who did; while I am not aware of a single instance of a High Churchman abandoning his own views to adopt those of the ultra-Protestant school.' After referring to the past services of the Evangelical party, the writer quotes the 'Times' newspaper of the day (1857) as saying 'that the High Church party *never was so numerous*, wealthy, fashionable, or enthusiastic as it is at the present day; and for every " Evangelical " bishop Lord Shaftesbury can make, there enter the Church *twenty curates, strong in the Fathers*, church building, vestments, seasons, and services.' He then proceeds: 'And this mighty influx of High Church principle amongst the inferior clergy is not only an index of what we may expect a little while hence, but an irresistible evidence of what has been achieved already. The decline of Evangelicalism, and the growth of Catholic tendencies, are the answer which I would give to writers like the one referred to in the " Dublin Review," whose argument against the feasibility of a corporate reunion is grounded on the hypothesis that the present numerical majority of Low Church men is likely to remain. *Those who know most of what is going on in the Anglican mind have come to a different conclusion*, and they anticipate that this majority, already so signally diminished, will at no distant day dwindle into a small minority, while the honest and fearless assertors of Anglican principles and Anglican practices will be so universal amongst the clergy and the intelligent and religious laity of the National Church, that we shall very soon see the statesmen and rulers of the land sensible of the change, and acting in compliance with it. I have already said that the reunion of Christians in the British empire, if ever attained, can only be brought about by the spontaneous rallying of all to the old paths and to the normal principles of Christianity, and not by the political triumph of any section over another. Let me then say that the issue I contemplate does not look to any struggle between High Churchmen and Evangelicals, *still less to any forcible ejectment of the latter from their position*. God forbid! Such an issue might involve the triumph of an idea, but it does not imply the union of men, or the victory of truth. What I look forward to is very different from this; it is to the gradual working of sound principles and sound argument; it is the awakening of men in general, who still agree in upholding Christianity, to the necessity of that moral and dogmatic unity which is essential to the progress and triumph of the system they profess to believe, and the only basis for a sound national system of instruction.'

The following passage, written nine years ago, sounds almost prophetic to us after the appearance of the 'Eirenicon':—

'And here let me express what I have long felt, that if ever, in the good Providence of God, the divisions that now rend asunder the Christian Church should be healed, that glorious result will be more due to the exertions and services of this truly learned and pious writer, Dr. Pusey, than to any other living man, while I cordially pray that God may preserve his valuable life to witness the full accomplishment of that to which his admirable writings have so much contributed, and that ere he close his honoured career, he may see Christendom what it was of old —one in Faith and one in Charity.'

The Essay concludes as follows: 'Should the Christian princes, who are now by God's mercy united in a general peace, agree with our Holy Father the Pope, that a General Council might be summoned for the restoration of religious unity, how glorious would be the result! *Never was there a period in the history of Christendom more favourable for the successful issue of such an enterprise.* The narrow prejudices of national feeling were never so powerless as at the present moment. The unprecedented intercourse of all nations with one another has tended to create a just appreciation of all that is good in each, while the continued interchange of kindness and hospitality has weakened old animosities and jealousies, making men remember, what Christianity had never ceased to inculcate, and what Christians ought never to have forgotten, that all mankind are brethren, children of a common Father, servants of the same God, and redeemed by the blood of the same Saviour; unity and fraternity are the very cry of the day, and although in the mouth of the Socialist and the Red Republican they assuredly mean something very different from what they symbolise in the mind of a Christian, yet even when uttered by the most frantic disciple of anarchy, they attest a deep and growing feeling, and express the utterance of that *vox populi* which all philosophy regards as prophetic, and the infallible harbinger of a divine visitation. On the other hand, our railways and our steamboats have annihilated distance; so that in a few days Paris or Rome might behold the meeting of the most august and venerable assembly that ever was held upon earth. What weighty subjects would be discussed! not only the religious but the political problems of the day might be solved, and with religious unity, the blessing of universal peace might be secured. The predictions of prophets, the visions of poets, and the unceasing cry of suffering humanity, would at last be realised and redressed, in the possession of that pearl of great price, the revealed truth of God, proclaimed by Jesus Christ, taught by the Apostles, and handed down in all ages by their successors in the Christian ministry, the Bishops of the Universal Church. . . . Let no man say that it is visionary to anticipate such a result. Even the infidel looks forward to a political millennium; but we Christians have " *a more sure word of prophecy,*" to which an inspired apostle reminds us that " *we do well to give heed.*"* We know that our Divine Founder prayed to His Father, that in the end all His followers might be brought to perfect unity, for what unity could be more perfect than that to which He referred as its type, " *even as He and the Father were one* "? † And that this unity was to be attained *on earth*, and not merely in the next life, He showed by what he added: " *that all men might believe that the Father had sent Him*; "† that is, that all ground for doubt and infidelity might be removed from mankind. Knowing, then, that our Lord prayed for this great and inestimable blessing, and remembering that other saying of His—" Heaven and earth shall pass away, but My word shall not fail "— we may look with confidence to the fulfilment of what still remains to be accomplished, arguing from what has been already fulfilled that the remainder also will surely come to pass.'

* 2 Pet. i. 19.   † John xvii. 21.

SYNOD OF CONSTANTINOPLE.

My citations from writers of the Oriental Church will be fitly opened with the following passage from a Letter signed by 'Joachim, Archbishop of Constantinople, New Rome, and Œcumenical Patriarch,' and the various Metropolitans and other Bishops forming the 'Synod of the Œcumenical Throne,' which appeared in the 'Union Chrétienne,' dated August 23, 1862:—

'Our Humility and the Holy Synod of Most Holy Metropolitans, our brothers and coadjutors in the Holy Ghost, having been informed, especially by your letter, of the Divine zeal which inflames you for the desired union of the Churches, are filled with spiritual joy. We crown your holy work with the most just praises, we pour forth for you the most ardent prayers, and we bestow with our whole heart on you and on your fellow-labourers our fullest benediction, Patriarchal and Synodal. And as we have seen with joy, in the letter of your piety, one Western and one Eastern priest united in the same love for the truth, joining their names as brethren, *so may we, one day,* by the grace of that God whose mercies are infinite, *behold the sister Churches of East and West embracing one another with sincerity and truth,* in the unity of the Spirit and in the bond of peace, in order that we may be One Body, and only one, in Jesus Christ, to the glory of the Father, the Son, and the Holy Ghost, the Most Holy and Undivided Trinity. His grace and benediction be with you.'

ARCHBISHOP OF BELGRADE.

My next extract is taken from a letter, dated December 10, 1862, addressed by 'Michael, Archbishop of Belgrade, and Metropolitan of all Servia,' to the Bishop of Oxford, and published at the time in the English newspapers:—

'Hitherto, consoling ourselves under every event of ill-fortune in the faith of Christ, received from the Apostles, by means of which we have become the heirs of the Holy Fathers, and which we have kept pure and undefiled to this very day; and firmly relying on the Author of the Hope which fails not, for a better lot to dawn upon our country, we do not and shall not cease to pour forth our prayers, as we are bidden by the precepts of the

Orthodox Church, *for the peace, and tranquillity, and reunion of Christendom*; and will earnestly entreat that the God of all grace will be pleased to gather together and restore His scattered flock in unity, and to bind them together in lasting concord. That those our just and lawful desires will at length be crowned with the most excellent success, we can the less doubt after hearing both thy letter, most beloved Brother in Christ, and that of thy most worthy fellow-Prelate of the See of London—a letter replete with the accents of gravity, authority, and, in fine, of help and safety, which I and my people receive with a thousand welcomes, as the dawn of a sun of Divine favour, which is about to rise upon our country.'

METROPOLITAN OF CORCYRA.

The following is from a letter to Dr. Fraser, an Anglican clergyman, from the Metropolitan of Corcyra:—

'Corcyra, the 10th November, 1864.

'REVEREND SIR,— With great gratification I received your letter of the 24th of October last, in which you were so kind as to communicate to me the information respecting the establishment of "The Eastern Church Association," in which you solicit me and my comprovincial Bishops to take part, and to enrol our names in the list of its patrons.

' I indeed am grateful for the honour which is proffered me, and at the same time I award the praise which is due to the said Association, which has undertaken this work well pleasing to God. And from my heart I pray that their pious purposes may have happy and favourable result. . . . . Believe me, that the Orthodox Eastern Church of Christ, which has continued always peaceable and very forbearing, and has never at any time injured other Christian Churches by proselytism or other means, unceasingly prays that the schisms of Churches being ended, and all heresy having died away, the innovations having been laid aside which have been introduced into very many of the Divine doctrines and sacraments, and the ancient customs and rites, the much-longed-for day may come in which all Christian Churches may be united into one, having one Head our Lord and God Christ Jesus, and for such a desirable unity the Orthodox Eastern Church makes request

fervently to God each day, in both her morning and her evening holy services. Imploring for you from God all that is good, I remain, your Reverence's humble servant, and one who earnestly prays to God for you, '✠ ATHANASIUS,
'Metropolitan of Corcyra.'

BISHOP OF EPHESUS.

The following is extracted from a Sermon by another Prelate of the Oriental Church, Paisius, Bishop of Ephesus, which appears in the Second Series of Reunion Sermons, p. 342. I give it as there translated from the original Greek, which I have not seen:—

'Having for no small period looked with constant anxiety for the origination of some distinguished and powerful assistance in the British Churches, towards setting forth, for the admiration of lookers-on, the holy principle of Unity instead of division, of love and a longing for restored communion in the place of misrepresentation and mischievous recrimination, we are deeply and sincerely rejoiced that a blessed beginning has been made through the Society there originated, which, by its devoted members, prays every sunrising for the very great blessing of Peace. In no spirit of *selfish independence do we regard our brethren of the West*, but, on the contrary, wheresoever we mark the rise or advance of such principles as have been set forth by our beloved in the Lord, the Bishops and Priests of the ancient Church of England, or others who have set themselves to work, we can feel no doubt that, by the assistance of God's Spirit, greater blessings will become apparent and appreciated, through the charitable intervention of this most commendable Society. . . . For no short period, likewise, have we constantly invoked the assistance of the Holy Spirit of God, to stir up in all Christians a desire for this. It is our usual petition and prayer in the Divine Liturgy, and our constant wish, constantly expressed, that the ministers of our Lord and Saviour should frequently utter aspirations for the same beneficial blessing. *This we desire, this we urge. Work undertaken in this spirit we bless.* And our benediction likewise is for and upon those alike, whether near us or far off, who follow the same Divine call, and constantly and charitably pray for the Union of the separated Churches.'

PRINCE ORLOFF.

Of the following letters from Prince Orloff, a distinguished lay member of the Russo-Greek Communion, the first appeared in the 'Times' of Dec. 28, 1865; the second, which supplements and explains it, in the 'Times' of Feb. 6, 1866:—

'We have been enabled to communicate the following extract from a private letter of Prince N. Orloff to M. Masloff:—

'"Belfontaine, near Fontainebleau, Nov. 28, 1865.

'"I promised to inform you of what occurred at the London meeting on the 15th inst. :—

'"The meeting was attended by about 80 persons, chiefly clergymen of High Church principles. Of the many eminent gentlemen present I will only mention the Bishop of Oxford, who presided, the Bishop of Lincoln, the Bishop-Coadjutor of Edinburgh, Drs. Pusey and Liddon, of Oxford; Dr. Williams, of Cambridge; and Mr. Wordsworth, the Dean [Canon] of Westminster. The Russians present were Father Yevgeni Popoff, our worthy chaplain in London; Count Alexei Tolstoi, and myself. The meeting was private. After reading the resolution of last year's meeting, purporting 'that the doctrine of the Eastern Church should be examined with a view to mitigating the estrangement of the various Christian Churches from each other,' the Bishop of Oxford desired me to say a few words. Having premised that I was speaking in a private capacity, I said that the Russian clergy, *praying daily for the establishment of a common Christian Church*, would be always inclined to promote it. In proof of this I alleged that the study of the English language had been introduced into our ecclesiastical academies, and that our clergy would be prepared to sift privately all disputed points. I added, however, that the most holy Philaret, the Archbishop of Moscow, and lofty patriarch of our Church, was of opinion that this was a grave and difficult question, which ought to be slowly matured, and, above all, investigated closely and minutely. In conclusion I moved:—

'" 1. That works should be published in England setting forth the history, doctrine, and present condition of the Anglican Church, with a view to proving that it is not a Protestant but a

Catholic Church, and, accordingly, related to the Eastern Church. I also remarked that the subject being altogether unknown to the Russian public, it ought to be explained fully and copiously.

'" 2. That Anglican clergymen sympathizing with the cause should be stationed at Moscow and S. Petersburg.

'" 3. That the matter should not be precipitated, or urged with too much eagerness or violence, but that we should trust in the Divine assistance rather than in the success of our human and short-sighted endeavours. What we had to do now was to prepare the ground by elucidating the question. The seed would grow up, and future generations, perhaps, would reap the harvest, if God willed it.

'" Father Popoff, who delivered an eloquent speech, breathing the spirit of Christianity, expressed himself to the same effect. After him some clergymen spoke on dogmatical points. I omit quoting their opinions; they will be probably communicated by Father Popoff in his report to the Chief Procurator of the Holy Synod. They had no immediate reference to the matter in hand. Ten Bishops, two Archbishops, and some other gentlemen, among whom was Mr. Gladstone, who was staying at Windsor with the Queen, had sent letters sympathising with our efforts. The Primus of Scotland observed in his letter that in 1718 the Scotch and Orthodox Churches had been negociating upon the subject when their discussions were suddenly interrupted by the death of Peter the Great, and the subsequent ascendency of Lutheran influences in Russia. The Bishops of Oxford and Edinburgh urged that, in their opinion, we should not content ourselves with preparing the ground, leaving the harvest to be reaped by future generations, but, deferring all dogmatical debates, proceed to celebrate the Lord's Supper by intercommunion, if such were the wish of the chiefs of our Church. Upon a gentleman remarking that Orthodox Christians might receive the communion in Anglican Churches even now, this was confirmed by the Bishops and Archbishops present, including the Primate of Canterbury. Another gentleman then stated that Englishmen were admitted to the Communion in the Orthodox Churches of Servia. Before the close of the debates I rose again to declare that the Russian Church being but one of the five branches of the Eastern Catholic Church, the matter was all the more complicated, and that the subordinate members of our clergy were not at liberty to decide any ecclesiastical questions, being entirely guided by the rules and directions of their Church. The Servian story, upon inquiry, proved a mere myth.*

' " Prayers were offered up at the beginning and close of the meeting, which had a purely spiritual character. No resolutions were passed, but all agreed *that the cause should be promoted cautiously, but incessantly.*

' " The day after I paid a visit to the Archbishop of Canterbury at his country seat. He would have liked to dispatch two bishops to Russia, but, hearing what I had to say against his plan, put it off. The Bishop of Exeter, the nonagenarian patriarch of the Anglican Church, also speaks with great interest of the work of reunion. The matter has nothing whatever to do with politics; though if a reunion were effected, the Russian and English interests in the East might possibly become identical.

' " PRINCE N. ORLOFF." '

' SIR,—Some misunderstanding having arisen from the publication of a private letter of mine, containing a very abridged account of the meeting which took place in London, on the 15th of November last, I consider it to be my duty towards my English friends to do my utmost in the following lines to clear up any doubts or misapprehension as to my views on this subject:—

' I have allowed a whole month to elapse in silence, with the view of ascertaining how the idea of intercommunion would be received by my fellow-countrymen, and I am most happy to be able to state that the Russian press *has greeted with the warmest of sympathy* the foreshadowing of a prospect of Christian unity so nobly put forward by the Eastern Church Association.

' Nothing could be more loyal and straightforward than the conduct of the learned and benevolent men assembled on that occasion was towards the Russians who came there.

---

* This has, I believe, been contradicted since by the clergyman referred to.

'They at once told us that they had no power or authority to engage the action of the Church of England in any way, each individual representing and giving utterance to his own private opinions only. I made a similar declaration in my own name and in that of my Russian friends. Therefore, no engagements, no illusory promises were made on either side, all of us being aware that the character of the meeting was to be perfectly informal, and that the sole object of the meeting was to try and ascertain by what means the Churches to which we severally belonged might some day be brought near together.

'Two distinct opinions were brought forward in the course of the discussion. Some members were in favour of immediate intercommunion, without waiting for dogmatic unity. Others felt that dogmatic unity must naturally precede intercommunion. All, however, were agreed upon one point—that it would be both useful and necessary to promote on both sides a careful study of the history and doctrine of the two Churches, and to work out as clearly as possible the wide extent of Gospel truth held by them both, as well as to limit and facilitate the discussion of all points of doctrine and practice on which they may differ.

'The impression left upon my mind by this meeting was that a deep feeling of Christian love had brought together persons of different countries assembled in Christ's name, who after some hours of conversation carried away with them the conviction that, let the results be what they might, they, at least, had fulfilled their duty as Christians in striving earnestly to find a means *for bringing nearer to each other two important and severed branches of the Church of Christ.*

'Personally, I need hardly say that I would not under any circumstances make religion a cloak for worldly or political ends, and that I consider such an *arrière pensée* as a sort of sacrilege; still less should I have thought of promoting a confederacy against another important branch of the Christian Church while uttering prayers and arguments in favour of concord and Unity.

'The very idea of Union (in a Christian spirit) would naturally exclude any such feelings, and, for my own, I can but re-echo the wish that not only Russian and English interests might become identical in the East, but *that the religious interests of the whole world might become so* for universal peace and the benefit of mankind.

'It has been insinuated that I was obliged to excuse myself, in the eyes of my own countrymen, for having participated in the prayers with which the meeting opened and closed. The Eastern Orthodox Church *has never forbidden its members from joining in any form of prayer with other Christians*, more especially with those who pray for "the peace of the whole world, and the union of divided Christendom."

'This insinuation is, therefore, totally devoid of foundation.

'Allow me, in closing these lines, to correct an error which appeared in my letter, and may possibly be of my own committing, though I cannot account for it.

'The Archbishop of Canterbury never expressed any intention to me of sending Bishops to Russia. It was rather a suggestion on my part that some learned Churchman might be induced to go there whenever the idea of intercommunion should attain a greater development; for in 1864 an eminent member of the Church of England had expressed to me his desire of visiting Moscow in order to sound the opinions of the Russian clergy, but abandoned his resolution on hearing from me how few among them were acquainted with the English language, and how little the question of intercommunion had been agitated at that time.

'I have the honour to be, Sir, your most obedient servant,

'PRINCE ORLOFF.'

'Brussels, Feb. 4.

It is worth observing that every one of these documents, some of them emanating from the very highest authorities of the separated Eastern Church, emphatically negative the popular but baseless error of supposing that she claims to be exclusively and by herself the One Catholic Church. No words could more explicitly assert the contrary.

BISHOP BARRINGTON.

We come lastly to the statements of Anglican writers on the restoration of Christian unity. The following passage, from a Charge delivered at the beginning of this century by Bishop Barrington, who then held the See of Durham, is very remarkable, when we consider the date, and the position of the writer. I give it as quoted in the Preface to the 'Book of Common Prayer,' published in 1815 by the Rev. Peter Gaudolphy, a Catholic priest, pp. vi.–viii. :—

'There appears to me to be in the present circumstances of Europe, better ground of hope for a successful issue to a dispassionate investigation of the differences which separate the two Churches of England and of Rome, than at any former period. With this view, and these hopes, I continue to exert my humble efforts in this great cause of charity and truth. And what public duty of greater magnitude can present itself to us, than the restoration of peace and union to the Church, by the reconciliation of two so large portions of it as the Churches of England and Rome? *What undertaking of more importance, and higher interest, can employ the piety and learning of the ministers of Christ, than the endeavour to accomplish this truly Christian work?* What more favourable period can occur than the present, when gratitude on one hand, and mutual interest on the other, prompt to such an accommodation? Gratitude, for valuable privileges already received; and mutual interest, in opposition to an overwhelming tyranny, equally hostile to all ecclesiastical establishments that are not yet subject to its infidel domination, which has at this time usurped, or is labouring to usurp, the domination of every State in Europe, except this happy country, so highly favoured by a protecting Providence. If I should live to see a foundation for such union well laid, and happily begun; if Providence should but indulge me with even a dying prospect of that enlargement of the Messiah's Kingdom, which we have reason to hope is not very remote, with what consolation and joy would it illuminate the last hours of a long life! With what heartfelt pleasure should I use the rapturous language of good old Simeon : "Lord, now lettest thou thy servant depart in peace." *May that Saviour, who has left us, in the record of His*

Gospel, His own anxious prayer for the union of His disciples, promote and prosper the blessed work of Catholic Union! And for this purpose, may He divest the minds of both Protestants and Catholics of all prejudice and passion, of all interested and uncandid views, and of every feeling contrary to the spirit of the Gospel. May He dispose all parties to make the Word of God the rule of their judgment and conduct; and so form the hearts of all to the simplicity of the Gospel, that, in all their endeavours for the good of the Church, their great purpose may be to seek Christ and Him crucified.'

BISHOP OF BRECHIN.

I give next the concluding words of a 'Charge' by one of the present Bishops of the Scotch Episcopal Church, who is also well known as a theological writer. It was delivered before 'The Annual Synod of the Diocese of Brechin,' Aug. 6, 1863 :—

'One cannot but feel that that is but an imperfect unity which does not comprehend the grand old Church of the East, so venerable in her traditions, so rigid in her maintenance of the deposit. That unity must be insufficient which, in view of the domination of the great Anglo-Saxon race, and its actual place in the civilisation of the world, has failed to touch the Church which, in its weakness and its strength alike, is the expression of its devotion and faith. Nor can a unity be said to be complete, which does not assimilate with itself all that is good and pious in the Protestant bodies. *In the face of the comparative failure of Christian missions, in view of the increasing infidelity of the thinking classes all over Europe, in regard to the low tone of Christian faith and practice through the world*, it cannot be said that by such unity as this the world believes that the Father sent the Son. No, my brethren, the deepest thinkers of the day are stretching forth to a unity which shall comprehend all the scattered members. They feel that *if the sixteenth century was one of dispersion, the nineteenth and the twentieth must be one of reunion*, if the Son of Man, when He cometh, is to "find *the* faith (as the original Greek is most correctly rendered) on the earth." While, on the one hand, opinions hitherto held in solution are being precipitated, and men are being called, as they never have been called before, to choose between a Christianity organised, hierarchical, dogmatic, and a scepticism implying sinful uncertainty of mind; on the other hand, as the means of locomotion are developed, and true Christian civilisation advances, *prejudices are being insensibly worn down, religious bitterness is giving way*, and men are coming to see that truth without love is an impossibility in the order of grace. And, as in the century preceding the Reformation, earnest men of all hues of opinion looked forward to the assembling of a General Council as the great cure of the evils of the day; so now may not we, laying to heart the great dangers we are in from our unhappy divisions, hope and labour and pray for the hour when the Church of God shall again come together in its glory and strength, when, compelled by the crushing assaults of the common foe, and *animated by the earnest desire of peace*, all who believe in the Divinity of our Blessed Saviour, and in the necessity of a visible Church as His organ, shall assemble under the guidance of God Himself; when every question shall be calmly discussed, every claim candidly weighed; when *misunderstandings shall be righted, logomachies explained*; when love shall hold the balance, and the Word of God be arbiter; when the Holy Ghost shall be present, and Christ Himself, as "our Peace," "shall send the rod of His power out of Zion," and, drawing all hearts to Himself, "will raise the tabernacle of David that is fallen, and close up the breaches thereof; and will raise up its ruins, and build it as in the days of old."' *

THE BISHOP OF SALISBURY.

The following is from 'A Charge, delivered by the Lord Bishop of Salisbury in his Cathedral, Aug. 11, 1864.' The quotation introduced into it from the Preface to Guizot's ' Meditations on the Christian Religion,' is important, as giving the judgment of a religious French Protestant, who is one of the most distinguished Continental statesmen and writers of the day:—

'Isolation! this indeed tells of our position as a Church, which, however necessary, however appointed for us, is associated with the thought of past corruptions, of some, perhaps undue, reliance on the arm of flesh, and of present weakness; and the

* Amos ix. 11.

consideration of it ought, therefore, to cause us sorrow, and yearnings for reunion with our separated brethren. And surely we may hope that the finger of God's Providence is, by our present troubles, pointing to this normal condition of the Body of Christ, *its unity*, as a means of escape from such troubles; surely we may almost dare to believe that the Saviour's prayer for the unity of the members of His body is taking effect through these late assaults on the common inheritance of Christendom, and *is preparing the hearts of men for communion with one another in one faith*, by placing them side by side in defence of some of its articles. . . . I think no one can have read the work of M. Renan * without feeling that he, by his infidel encroachments on the inheritance which we share with the Church of France, has, by creating that sympathy which attends upon a united resistance to a common danger, contributed something towards removing the barriers which have long parted us from that celebrated communion, and so towards awaking in the universal Church the blessed spirit of " truth, unity, and concord." Be it ours never to forget the solemn words of Count de Maistre : " If Christians should ever draw towards each other—*and every consideration might urge them to do so*—it seems that the first advance would most naturally be made by the Church of England." The attempts which Convocation has sanctioned to enter into friendly relations with the Eastern Church synchronise, we cannot but observe, with our late controversies. And it is to these same assaults which God has, in His Providence, permitted men to make on the faith, that we owe the following strong warning with which M. Guizot has very lately prefaced his 'Meditations on the Essence of the Christian Religion' :—
" It is in fact the whole Christian Church, and not this or that Christian Church in particular, which is at the present day the object of attack in its fundamental principles. When the Supernatural, the Inspiration of the sacred Books, and the Divinity of our Lord Jesus Christ, are denied, the blow falls upon all Christians, whether Catholics, Protestants, or Greeks; and all Christians, whatever may be their private grounds of disagreement from each other, or their forms of Church government, are robbed of the very bases of their faith. And it is by their faith that all the Churches of Christ maintain their life. There is no descrip-

* The *Vie de Jesus* had appeared that year.

tion of civil government, be it monarchy or republic, be it centralised or shared by many local authorities, which is equal to the work of upholding a Church. There is no authority so strong, no freedom so broad and wide, as to be able to take the place and do the work of faith in a religious society. For *the unity of a Church is the union of souls, and it is a common faith which really binds souls together.* When, then, the foundations of their common faith are assailed, differences which may exist between Christian Churches on particular questions, or points of contrast in their organisation and government, come to possess only a secondary interest, since Churches have to protect themselves against a danger common to each and all, when the spring which supplies each one of them with the draught of life is itself threatened with exhaustion."'

The Bishop proceeds to observe that 'an English Churchman' will be unable to agree with M. Guizot as to the 'secondary importance of questions which affect the constitution of the Church of Christ,' but that he would not, therefore, forego the pleasure of quoting a passage ' in which the present perils of Christendom are so forcibly described by so high an authority.'

I subjoin the following passage from a published Letter of the Bishop, dated Jan. 23, 1865, in reply to a small minority of his clergy who had objected to some statements in the Charge :—

'I have nothing more to add by way of explanation. But here, at the conclusion of my answer, I must again testify that *it is the desire of our Lord that His Church should be one*—that *it is the duty of all His members to bring their minds into harmony with the mind of Him Who is their Head*—that those who, whatever be their differences, are in the presence of a common danger, though they do not by this acquire, and so should not seek, any condonation for wrong teaching, should recognise in this fellowship a claim for unity; and, lastly, that they who support this claim for unity, without giving, at the same time, all those details of an Irenicon, which are to guide and control any reawakened feelings for Reunion, are not to be charged with a readiness to sacrifice the truth of God for the indulgence of morbid longings and ill-regulated affections in a communion of error, but should, as far as the inalienable rights of truth allow it, be sheltered from misconstruction by that charity "which hopeth all things."'

BISHOP OF CAPETOWN.

I take the following from a Charge delivered at Capetown in 1865 by Bishop Gray, which was reported in the 'Guardian' newspaper:—

'It is very significant that open assaults upon the faith, if they have not created a yearning for closer union among the several members of Christ, have at least been accompanied by efforts after the attainment of so great a blessing. Ours, if it is an age of religious discussion, is also an age of drawing together. I have ever looked with interest upon the proceedings of the Evangelical Alliance, though based, as I think, upon an essentially wrong principle, because I have regarded its formation as the expression of a conviction that our present state is a wrong one, and ought not to be persevered in. Its work is a preparatory work. It may *pave the way* for future reunion and organisation in our body. It can never become a *substitute* for the unity of the Church. *Organisation is essential to joint action.* . . . What *a waste of strength* is there through disunion! Two are required, where divisions exist, to do the work which might be wrought by one; and these work not with, but against, each other. The very cost alone of multiplied agencies is a witness against the schisms which have made them needful. The jealousies, rivalries, estrangements, embitterments, which are the necessary fruits of division, ever threaten the success of all undertakings, and bid fair to work out the fulfilment of the prophetic warning, "If ye bite and devour one another, take heed that ye be not consumed one of another." It is the conviction that these things are so— that the state of the followers of Christ is not what their Lord prayed that it might be; that it is injurious to His cause whom they love; *hinders the growth of the life of God within the individual soul and in religious communities,* and even threatens the overthrow of the faith—that is leading many in our day to express their longings for a restoration of unity, and to labour for its accomplishment. . . . Are not all these things tokens for good? Do they not indicate a very wide-spread and deep-seated conviction that *a divided state is a wrong state*; that true believers in Christ should not remain for ever in a state of alienation from each other, but should search after some basis for union among themselves? May these convictions spread wider and wider as years pass on, among ourselves and throughout Christendom! May the Comforter descend with healing on His wings, and unite all the followers of a common Master in one household and body and Church, holding and embracing the "one Lord, one Faith, one Baptism, one God and Father of us all!" Our prayers, my brethren, should be directed to this end; *our daily intercessions should be offered for the restoration of lost unity among ourselves, and throughout Christendom.* We should strive, amid our manifold divisions, to give as little offence as may be to those who are separated from us. *If the restoration of unity be the condition of the conversion of the world, every sacrifice but that of truth must be made to attain it.'* *

REV. W. J. E. BENNETT.

The following passage, at the close of a published Sermon on 'Many Members but One Body,' 'preached on the Feast of Pentecost, 1865, in the Parish Church of Frome Selwood,' by the Vicar, Mr. Bennett, contains some generous admissions. With one suggestion, at least, we shall all be ready to sympathise :—

'The confession of error belongs to all. *Our* Bishops and Pastors did certainly deal with the Church as they found her at the Reformation, with miserable misunderstandings. I think the Bishops and Pastors on the other side may be placed, without breach of charity, in the same condemnation. If they who have succeeded to their places would but recall the ancient love which they once bore to us, would relax some of those points of discipline which have grated upon the English character—for instance, the celibacy of the clergy; restore some of the privileges of the Church which, in times of antiquity, were never denied to the people—for instance, the administration of the chalice; if they would make such generous allowances for the national characteristics of different people and different ages, as true Catholicity

---

* This last sentence is almost a verbal repetition of the words of the late Archbishop Murray in the MS. letter already referred to: 'On our side, as the instruments of the Most High for preaching peace to men of good will, *we should leave nothing undone, short of sacrificing truth, towards uniting divided Christendom.'* Such language is worthy the lofty character of the writers and their high office in their respective hierarchies. May it become the watchword of all their brethren!

would seem to demand; and, more than all, if they would learn that there are multitudes of faithful children of the Church in this country, tired and weary with the strife of tongues, longing for the smile of returning friendship and brotherhood, broken only by the misunderstandings of the past, *they would at least pray for such a time* as God, in His mercy, might bring about, when the schism of past ages might be reunited, and the discord of party spirit might be healed.' He quotes St. Cyprian, and thus concludes: 'It is this truth; the Church which alone holds this truth; this one great Universal Church which we long to see among us, and feel again, and worship in again; not the Roman, not the Greek, not the English. Away with all such party distinctions, such *local and national* peculiarities. The Church, which is the Church of all, is alone the Church of God.'

REV. T. T. CARTER.

My next extract is from a very remarkable Sermon by the Rev. T. T. Carter, Rector of Clewer, one of the most respected leaders of the Catholic party in the Church of England, preached at All Saints, Margaret Street, 'On the Eighth Anniversary of the A. P. U. C.' 1865, and since published under the title of 'The Future Unity of The Christian Family.'*

'It is not the way in which Unity is to be restored with which we are concerned, but the conditions of mind which are required in us, and throughout the Church, in order that there may be no resistance to the working of the Spirit Who, abiding as from the beginning within the whole Body, as the outer frame of His indwelling Presence, is ever tending to renew the original Unity in which He first formed it. Our responsibilities and our powers extend to cherishing the spirit most favourable to Reunion;

---

* In a note at p. 4 an extract is given from a letter of 'one of the original Roman Catholic founders of the Association' which the preacher, with his permission, read from the pulpit. 'May I request you to present my warmest assurance of continued sympathy in the holy work of the Corporate Reunion of the three great bodies of divided Christendom, for which I shall never cease to labour according to my ability? . . . I firmly believe that the Court of Rome will sooner or later enter warmly into the great movement for corporate reunion—it being always understood that such a reunion is based upon the orthodox profession of every Article of Catholic Faith.'

beyond this we cannot pass. The overruling of events, the changes of feeling and opinion in the mind of the Church, the ordering of the chain of Providences, by which the complex web of confusion may be unravelled and reknit in order—all such issues are in the Hand of God. We are not, however, any the less to be stirred to the desire of Reunion because we cannot see the way of its accomplishment. We are not the less to offer prayer for its being granted to us, because the difficulties may seem to be insurmountable. *The accomplishment of a restoration of Unity is really not more difficult to imagine, than was the possibility of its loss.* The one would have seemed on the day of Pentecost not more improbable than the other appears in our own day. The first disciples went forth as one Spirit; they must have been startled to find the Babel brood of heresy spring up within their own company. We go forth with the din of conflicting opinions everywhere around us; the very misery and weariness of disunion may itself tend to the universal desire for unity and peace. It would be scarcely more improbable than that the blessedness of that first peace, sustained by the full power of the One Spirit, should have been so soon lost. The events which may at some future day lead to any reproduction of that first love, wholly inscrutable as they are, are beyond our power. "The lot is cast into the lap, but the whole disposing thereof is of the Lord."* But we need not the less rejoice to turn aside from the harassment of controversy, to dwell for awhile on thoughts which will, by God's blessing, tend to peace, and induce us to foster, at least in our own hearts, the unity and love so precious in the sight of God.

'And with this view before me, the point which I would urge, the only clear practical one, is this—that *there are conditions of mind necessarily to be wrought in us, if we would share the spirit which conduces to Unity, conditions of mind directly tending to its restoration,* which it must therefore be of the utmost moment for us to cherish, because every one of us must surely give account before God, how his own soul is disposed in regard to them, since He desires Unity for His Church, and He will surely shed a special blessing on those who put no hindrance in

---

* Prov. xvi. 33.

its way, or rather by their words and works, as far as in them lies, seek to promote it. Let us consider, therefore, some of these spiritual conditions of which we must one day give account before God, and on which the hope of the returning of the grace of Unity essentially depends. . . . Again, a second condition of mind necessary for the promotion of Unity, is the largeness of heart, which can apprehend the largeness of the Divine design working itself out in the narrow earthen vessel of the Visible Church. The truth which embraces all possible phases of Humanity must needs be greater than any age or any race. The immensity of the Godhead revealed to the mind of the Church must be greater than the Church. Consider the generations which it required to elaborate any one series of dogmas, as, e.g., those relating to our Blessed Lord's Nature, separating the truth from manifold errors, and fixing in unchangeable moulds the forms of truth on this one particular portion of the Church's Creed. Expand this process of the settlement of truth to the whole compass of the Divine revelation, and *calculate what would be required for the elaboration of all its treasures*. Again, consider how to one race of mankind, gifted with its own special genius, as distinct from that of other races, has been given the working out of one portion of the complex whole, to another another portion; how, e.g., to the Eastern mind exclusively was consigned the working out of the problems affecting the Godhead in Its union with Humanity—the theology, properly speaking, of the Catholic Creed. Then see what important results flow from this fact as to the necessity of the different minds of the different races of mankind for the composition of the entireness of the truth, as affecting all the relations between God and man, the embracing all the effects of the vast revelation on all the phases of human life.

'And we can surely trace in the past history of the Church *this progressive development,* through the instrumentality of different races, *of different portions of the Faith.* . . . Meanwhile our practical duty is clear. To be gentle and forbearing, to overcome prejudices, *to clear up misunderstandings whether in one's own mind, or in the minds of others,* to make large allowances for variety of conditions, to reverence God wherever the trace of His footsteps can be discerned on the dark waters, to be ever ready to acknowledge error while sacredly upholding the soul's convictions of truth, to hope all things, to remember how Angels and Saints now at rest regard the controversies of this lower world while they look on His Face Who is Truth, and marvel at our contentions about its modes of expression in earthly forms, to catch their spirit as we contemplate them, and learn to look with their eyes on the same vision, and see all questions as they are reconciled in God—moreover and above all, *to live the life of the spirit of our Creed*, and to seek to draw nearer to each other in the sameness of a saintly mind, that thus holding unceasing communion in the same spirit, we may more nearly apprehend the Truth under the same aspects—and together with all this to mourn before God our own and our brethren's sins, which have widened the sad breach, and to trust to the compassion of God to grant for the sake of the merits of our dearest Lord what our utmost efforts in themselves must fail to accomplish,—such are among the signs which God approves as marking a true love of Unity.

'Too much stress is often laid on the length of time which has elapsed since the divisions, as though in the power of renewing grace time was to be heeded. "Beloved, be not ignorant of this one thing, that one day is with the Lord as a thousand years; and a thousand years as one day."[*] The revolution of a life in the conversion of a soul causes the past, however long, to be as though it had never been. Is grace different in Churches than in individuals? *The Reunion of the Faithful is a certainty of the Divine predestination.* It will be granted within the veil, if not without. But *the unceasing Intercession of our Lord is evidently pleading for the accomplishment of this blessed restoration in this world.* He regards it as the necessary fulness of the proof of His own mission. He prays not merely for the first disciples, but for them also which shall believe on Him through their word, "that they all may be One, as Thou Father art in Me, and I in Thee, that they also may be One in Us." And the reason given marks the reference of this desire to the earthly condition of the Church, as His witness, "that the world may believe that Thou hast sent Me."'[†]

---

[*] 2 Pet. iii. 8.   [†] John xvii. 21.

GLADSTONE.

My quotations from Anglican writers will be fitly brought to their conclusion with the testimony of our great statesman, the glory of Oxford and of England, who holds much the same position as a zealous layman towards the Anglican Church, which Montalembert (whose words I have quoted in this Letter) holds towards the Catholic Church in France. And his testimony is the more remarkable as occurring in a work published twenty-six years ago, before the appearance of Tract 90 and the literature it evoked, and when very few, even of the most thoughtful and far-sighted of the Tractarian party, were beginning to recognise the importance or contemplate the attainment of union with the rest of Christendom. The following passages occur at pp. 504, 505, 507, 508, 514, 515, of his 'Church Principles' (1840) :—

'In spite of all that men say loosely or perversely against the duty and need of visible union, there is evidently a latent sense of that duty and that need (which is more deeply seated in our instincts than in our clear consciousness), wherever the Christian faith has been inwardly received and retained. We perceive this instinct of truth battling, though unequally, with false argumentation, oftentimes reviving, and hardly anywhere to be altogether extinguished. We see it qualifying the irregularities to which zeal is liable, emerging, though disguised, in efforts for partial reunions, such as that recently effected between the Scottish Church establishment and one of the bodies of Presbyterian Dissenters in that country; and also like that attempted very recently between certain classes of Dissenters—I believe the Independents and Baptists—of this country, and the corresponding bodies in America. We see it dictating, indirectly, many of the reproaches now uttered against Church doctrine, by producing a soreness that can hardly be accounted for, except by a sense that something is wrong. There is then, and God be thanked for it, yet remaining a strong though indistinct sentiment *in favour of visible unity among Christians*; and wherever it may be found, and under whatever conditions, let it be nursed and husbanded as a sacred store, until the day come when it may be profitably exercised and dispensed for the attainment of its object. . . . *That unity is valuable we are agreed*, at least sufficiently for the present purpose. . . . It is easy to say, this is distant, this is difficult, this is visionary and chimerical. The two first I readily admit; but when the mind recurs to that most solemn prayer of the Saviour, at that most solemn hour, for the visible unity of His Church, I feel how impossible it is to wrench away the hope of this (however distant and however difficult) achievement from the heart of all true belief in Christ, *with which it is*, as we have seen, *vitally and inseparably intertwined.* . . . There is in the minds of serious persons a growing sentiment that the powers and principles of absolute unbelief are spreading more and more widely; and while in their most extended operations they are, by whatever diversity of means, gradually sapping the specifically preservative or Catholic principles in the greater number of Christian communities indiscriminately, they are likewise gathering increase of strength, and taking form and body, and indicating symptoms of systematic preparation for the attack upon all belief in Divine revelation. There is a deep and growing, though a reluctant conviction, that if, and so far as victory may be destined to infidelity, it will be achieved through the weakness infused into the opposite principle by our religious divisions. The first impulse is to union for the sake of determined resistance. It is clear that we are weakened by division, and that, even at the best, we could have no strength to spare. It is felt that there are, after all, strong sympathies among all believers in the Person and Sacrifice of Christ, *could they but be extricated, combined, and embodied.* And as in the probable advance of events, human will becomes more and more emancipated from extraneous restraints, and as the development of all good and of all evil principles becomes more and more free and energetic, the need of union will be more felt among the believers in revealed religion; and the duty will perhaps at length appear so legible to all, that *we shall wonder we could ever be indifferent upon the subject, or otherwise than most keenly alive to its practical importance.*' *

* Since this Letter was sent to press, a friend has called my attention to the following remarkable passage on Reunion, by Professor Goldwin Smith, occurring in a letter to the *Daily News* of Nov. 20, 1861, and reprinted in the second edition of *Lectures on the Study of History* (Parker, 1865), pp. 180, 181. I gladly avail myself of the testimony of so profound and religious a thinker to the conclusions I have insisted upon, while he approaches the subject from a point of view in some respects widely differing from my own:

With these weighty words of one of the deepest and most religious thinkers of our age and country, I bring my extracts to an end. And may He, the Spirit of Truth, who proceedeth from the Father and the Son, who is the Bond of Unity in the Persons of the Undivided Trinity, and maketh men to be of one mind in an house, vouchsafe to bless this little work for the honour of our Risen Lord and the peace of those who love Him, not according to the writer's poor deserts, but according to the fulness of His sevenfold gifts, who is Himself the Gift of the Most High! May He anoint with the Pentecostal fire of charity the hearts of all who worship Him, within or without the pale of His earthly Church, and the Saints in light who stand before His Throne above, and enrich their tongues with utterance to 'pray for the peace of Jerusalem,' that those who own ' One Lord, One Faith, One Baptism,' may have ' One Fold, and One Shepherd,' that all may be one in Him!

' A greater object of endeavour than any mere political emancipation or improvement begins to present itself to our view. . . . The reunion of Christendom, which for three centuries has been an empty and hopeless prayer, *is likely at last to become a practical aim.* Probably it would be a greater service to humanity, on philosophical as well as religious grounds, *to contribute the smallest mite towards this consummation,* than to construct the most perfect demonstration of the free personality of man. As things are, rationalism and fatalistic reveries may be laboriously confuted; but amidst the energies and aspirations of a regenerated Christendom, *they would spontaneously pass away.*'

www.ingramcontent.com/pod-product-compliance
Lightning Source LLC
Chambersburg PA
CBHW030353170426
43202CB00010B/1355